DATE DUE

DEMCO 38-296

PREPARING
· F · O · R ·
ACCREDITATION

A
HANDBOOK
FOR
ACADEMIC
LIBRARIANS

PATRICIA ANN SACKS
SARA LOU WHILDIN

AMERICAN LIBRARY ASSOCIATION
CHICAGO AND LONDON 1993

Text design by Diana Ankerman

Composed by Publishing Services, Inc. in Korinna
and Palacio on Xyvision/Cg8600

Printed on 50-pound Finch Opaque, a pH-neutral
stock, and bound in 10-point C1S cover stock by
IPC, St. Joseph, MI

The paper used in this publication meets the minimum
requirements of American National Standard for
Information Sciences—Permanence of Paper for Printed
Library Materials, ANSI Z39.48–1984. ∞

Library of Congress Cataloging-in-Publication Data

Sacks, Patricia Ann.
    Preparing for accreditation : a handbook for
academic librarians / by Patricia Ann Sacks &
Sara Lou Whildin.
        p.   cm.
    Includes bibliographical references.
    ISBN 0-8389-0621-4 (alk. paper)
    1. Academic libraries—United States—Evaluation.
2. Universities and colleges—United States—
Accreditation.   I. Whildin, Sara Lou.
II. Title.
Z675.U5S146   1993
027.7'0973—dc20   93-19712

Printed in the United States of America.

97 96 95 94 93   5 4 3 2 1

Contents

Preface

In her 1973 Doubleday novel, *A State of Grace*, Joy Williams writes, "It's difficult to tell at the end of the day whether it was theory or need that got you through it." That's how most people in the academy feel at the conclusion of accreditation and other comprehensive assessment processes. Librarians are no exception. They and their colleagues swear, "Next time will be different." There won't be misplaced reports, lost and meaningless data, eleventh hour writing and data analysis exercises, the last minute frenzy. To ward off desperation, they seek out both theoretical and practical advice to prepare for "next time." And on campuses with a number of accredited programs, another review may be "just around the corner."

Academic librarians have sought such advice from the Association of College and Research Libraries, and have been referred to the Standards and Accreditation Committee or the recently developed list of accreditation consultants. As a former chair of the Committee, Pat Sacks frequently responds to pleas for help in preparing for accreditation. At the urging of former committee members and a succession of ACRL staffers, she joined with Sara Whildin to develop this Handbook that librarians can consult in preparing for formal accrediting reviews. The Handbook is founded on goal-based theory, but moves beyond theory to address the need for practical organizational advice, and user-focused assessments.

Acknowledgments

A number of people and organizations have supported the development of this handbook. They include The Association of College and Research Libraries, especially its Standards and Accreditation Committee. We have benefited greatly from the ideas and help of the following people who read the manuscript and offered comments during its development: Herb Bloom, Mary Ellen Davis, Susan Kroll, Leslie Manning, and David Walch.

Many of the advisories in this manual reflect the authors' experiences of serving on a score of accrediting teams, learning about the institutions' and their libraries' accomplishments and responding to their needs. They also arise from Strategic Planning and Accrediting Steering Committee memberships (two as chairperson), and the wisdom and insights of our campus colleagues. We are honored to have had the contributions, support and patience of the Library Staffs at Cedar Crest and Muhlenberg Colleges and the Delaware County Campus of Pennsylvania State University.

While many have contributed to this Handbook, it is successful only if you—the reader—find it useful. We seek your feedback and suggestions for improvement. Please let us know what works and what doesn't. You can contact us at the addresses on the comment form at the back of the Handbook.

Introduction

Purpose

This is a "how to" book. Its purpose is to assist academic libraries in preparing for the reviews of external agencies responsible for accrediting their colleges or universities. Librarians who are responsible for conducting such reviews will find suggestions on how to set up the accrediting review project and proceed through its phases. Organizations commonly set up review teams to review their operations, solve problems, and pursue new developments. The handbook may also be helpful to those libraries conducting goal-based program reviews and assessments as the characteristics of these reviews approximate those of the accrediting review. This handbook advises the library to become involved in accrediting reviews as part of its ongoing efforts of self-study and assessment. As such, the review can be planned, organized, staffed, funded, evaluated, and reported—in short managed like any other library project or function. Our approach to accrediting events is that while they are major undertakings in the life of the academic institution, they are a component of the overall planning, self-study, and assessment processes.

The focus of this handbook is on management processes, rather than on specific accrediting agency policy or program review requirements. As such, the handbook does not replace the standards, guidelines, manuals, checklists, or other documents of the accrediting agencies or professional associations. Accrediting agency and professional association documents usually describe value-centered criteria, and standards and procedures for conducting accrediting reviews. The library undergoing an accrediting agency's review will want to acquire and study the agency's standards and "how to" materials, and use them in conducting its study and reporting data and results. This handbook will help the library work with a specific accrediting agency's materials and develop responses that provide positive outcomes satisfying its clientele and accrediting requirements.

Although the primary audience for this handbook is the academic librarian with little experience in accreditation or program assessments, veterans of these processes may find selected sections helpful in reviewing the organizational tasks associated with accrediting team visits, or in identifying input-output measures appropriate to evaluation processes.

Goal-Based Evaluation

This handbook employs the goal-based approach to assessment, which is the model employed by accrediting agencies and professional library association standards. In goal-based assessment, the library asks itself if its goals address its mission and whether its programs and activities achieve these goals. A goal is developed in response to the question, "What does the library want to accomplish?" and it proceeds to an assessment of "How well does it do it?" For example, if the goal is to teach students how to find information relevant to their needs, the library will be looking for evidence of student comprehension and successful application of the skills needed to find this information. The design of goal-based assessment may be simple or complex, but most structures include these elements:

- Identifying the goals and objectives of the program under review.
- Defining the accrediting agency's criteria and standards that apply to the program to be assessed.
- Knowing the campus climate and the incentives for participating in accrediting review activities.
- Involving library users. Involvement includes early, active participation of students and faculty who are the end users and who will be affected by the results.
- Involving key administrators in setting and reaffirming goals and supporting the process.
- Deciding what meaningful information to collect. Three questions are critical:
    Why does the library need this information?
    What use will the library make of this information?
    How can the library support the collection and analysis
        process?

- Collecting the data and information, and analyzing and interpreting the results.
- Writing a concise, readable report that clearly describes and analyzes library programs. The report should recommend improvements, priorities, an action agenda, and implementation schedules.
- Communicating the findings.
- Using the findings in making decisions about quality, improvements, and priorities.
- Evaluating the accrediting experience to refine the library's ongoing assessment program.

While the analysis assesses the degree of congruence between goals and performance, the focus is on interpreting program performance, exploring the reasons for the results, and taking responsibility for the use of the findings. A key component of this responsibility is a communication process that builds ownership and involvement in the accrediting review. It requires early, active participation of the library's constituencies who will be affected by or involved with using the findings. The support of individuals who have high credibility and serve as opinion leaders can be critical. These individuals can create a climate of trust and support for the accrediting process. The complexities of communication and user involvement are less recognized in the accrediting agencies' guidelines but require significant staff energies and time. Communication with the institution's constituencies is never finished. The handbook offers practical advice and suggestions for developing effective involvement processes.

Handbook Organization

The handbook is organized into four chapters.

Chapter One, *The Accrediting Environment,* provides an overview of the accreditation landscape and the role of the academic library in the process. It is a useful context for the library unfamiliar with the accrediting process.

Chapter Two, *Accrediting Practices and Procedures,* describes how accrediting reviews are conducted and the procedures followed at both the institutional and library levels, such as planning, staffing, scheduling, and reporting. It is modeled on the practices most frequently employed by accrediting agencies and their affiliated institutions.

Chapter Three, *Preparing for the Accreditation Review,* concentrates on the tools of any accreditation review. These tools are the mission and goals of the library and their relationship to the mission and goals of the parent institution, performance evaluation (including input and output measures), and organizational skills. It provides practical assistance in developing and implementing an accrediting review program which assesses the library's achievements.

Chapter Four, *Using Accreditation Results*, discusses the results of the process, responses to the agency reports, addressing performance deficits, change agents, and continuing the evaluation process. Good management and the cultivation of an environment that enlists the support of library staff and library users guide our efforts in using results and effecting change.

Sample documents and worksheets are included in several chapters. Each chapter concludes with a list of selected readings.

Chapter One The Accrediting Environment

Purpose

Accreditation is a voluntary, self-regulatory process for encouraging and assisting institutions of higher education to evaluate and improve their educational endeavors. It identifies publicly those institutions and programs that meet established qualifications and standards as determined through initial and periodic evaluations. The Council on Postsecondary Accreditation (COPA), which recognized accrediting bodies meeting COPA's provisions and procedures, defined postsecondary accreditation as:

> a process by which an institution or a specialized unit of postsecondary education periodically evaluates its educational activities and seeks an independent judgment by peers that it achieves substantially its own educational objectives and meets the established standards of a body from which it seeks accreditation. Generally the accreditation process involves (1) a clear statement of the institution's or unit's objectives, (2) a self-study by the institution or unit which examines its activities in relation to those objectives, (3) an on-site evaluation by a selected group of peers which reports to the accrediting body, and (4) a decision by this independent body that the institution or unit does or does not meet its standards for accreditation.
>
> *COPA Glossary*

Basically, the purposes of the process are to improve educational quality, insure institutional integrity, and serve the public interest. The outcomes are responsible professional assessments about the effectiveness of an educational institution in terms of the institution's stated objectives and their appropriateness to its nature and condition. These assessments are based on the institution's mission and goals—on how well it does what it says it is doing. The peer review (a visiting team report), and the accrediting agency's action (accredit, reaccredit, and qualifying conditions) are communicated promptly to the institution. The institution in turn will tell its constituents about the report and the accrediting agency's action. Accrediting bodies keep confidential the information they receive, and disclose action with respect to an individual institution prejudicial to its good standing only when the evidence clearly indicates that the public interest will be served by such disclosure.

Type of Accrediting Agencies

The landscape includes three types of accrediting bodies: holistic, specialized, and state agencies. The holistic agencies deal with the college or university as a whole and focus on institution-wide mission and goals as central to the institution's existence and purpose. From each institution's definition of these central aspects flows an assessment program that provides the evidence of its achievements, and enables it to use the results to sustain and improve its performance. The holistic agencies include the six regional accrediting associations:

Middle States Association of Colleges and Schools

New England Association of Schools and Colleges

North Central Association of Colleges and Schools

Northwest Association of Schools and Colleges

Southern Association of Colleges and Schools

Western Association of Schools and Colleges

Other accrediting agencies whose scope is "the total institution" are organizations such as the National Association of Trade and Technical Schools that accredits proprietary institutions, or the American Association of Bible Colleges whose members are church-related colleges and universities.

The specialized accrediting agencies review selected programs, apply criteria related to a profession or occupation, and assess the quality of its practice. Appropriate standards are upheld in the interests of the profession and for the good of society. Specialized accreditation regards that mission as its function. Most specialized accrediting bodies accredit "first professional degree" programs at the level that may apply at a particular college or university. Specialized accrediting agencies include the American Assembly of Collegiate Schools of Business, the National League of Nursing, National Council for the Accreditation of Teacher Education, the American Bar Association, and the Council on Social Work Education.

States have the responsibility of chartering or incorporating institutions of higher education and authorizing them to operate. The extent to which the states monitor colleges and universities within their borders varies to a great degree. Some state agencies cover only the public sector or its segment while others have the authority in the independent sector as well. State-level review is an exception to the voluntary regional or professional agencies that are major evaluative forces. The states' involvement in academic program review has expanded during the past fifteen years to satisfy the accountability requirements of various constituencies and to allocate limited funds to address state-defined priorities.

To get to know each of the three major types of accrediting agencies, a description of their prominent features and organizational structures follows.

Institutional Associations

The institutional associations, including the six regional associations, are organizations of member institutions with governing bodies elected by the membership. These associations develop policies and procedures for the accreditation of colleges and universities. They decide on accreditation status and assist affiliated institutions to assess and improve their programs and sustain their levels of achievement. Membership meetings provide forums for open and candid discussions of common concerns, the diversity of experiences and key challenges of the future. They enable action on proposed standards and guidelines documents.

To achieve their purposes the associations employ an accreditation process with the following features:

- Institutional self-study involving representatives of the institution's constituencies and culminating in a report that constitutes a realistic planning document.
- On-site evaluation by a team of professional peers that reports its recommendations to the institution and the accrediting association's governing board. The team's assessments focused on "how well the institution does what it says it is doing" are communicated promptly to the institution.
- Institutional responses to reports of the team. These responses include communication with the accrediting agency and informing its constituents of the findings of the team's report.
- Action on accreditation by the association's governing board.

• Procedures for institutional appeal of a governing board decision.

The institutional associations monitor the college's or university's condition in annual and special topic reports submitted to the association by the accredited institution. If an institution contemplates a significant change, e.g., initiating a graduate program, developing off-site educational programs, mergers, or changing mission, it is required to report such change to the association. It then undergoes a special review to assure its ability to achieve its purposes at a satisfactory level.

The association employs a staff that assists a member institution in the following ways:

• Developing papers and manuals amplifying the agency's standards. These publications that are designed to offer assistance to its members cover topics such as mission and goals setting, assessing student academic achievement, outcomes, off-campus programs, and planning.

• Conducting workshops for member institutions to assist them to plan and prepare for self-studies and reports.

• Training evaluation team members.

• Counseling on the self-study design and supporting requirements, the selection and use of assessment instruments, and the preparation for ongoing, follow-up studies.

• Reviewing association standards and procedures with faculty, administrators, trustees, and students.

• Assisting the institution to inform its constituencies of the association's standards and procedures and to address the results of self-study and evaluation.

• Communicating with its members via newsletters and journals.

Because most accrediting bodies have small staffs, they focus on the identification and promotion of their standards and assistance during the self-study preceding an on-site evaluation. An institution is formally visited only every five to ten years unless it is experiencing difficulties or undergoing rapid change. The institution's annual or periodic reports play controlling roles in self-regulation.

Specialized Associations

The more than fifty professional or specialized accrediting agencies recognized by the former Council on Postsecondary Accreditation perform a self-regulatory function for specific programs, disciplines, or schools within a college or university. The fields covered by these agencies include teacher education, medicine, nursing, medical technology, law, social work, business, journalism, mortuary science, dentistry, art, architecture, engineering, and engineering technology. One-half of the programs covered by these agencies employ certification, licensing, or other examinations that are dimensions of the accrediting process.

The standards for specialized accreditation commonly include statements on the organization and governance of the program, faculty qualifications and teaching loads, admission and retention of students, curriculum and course descriptions, library resources, facilities and equipment, and financial support. Many specialized agencies often require accreditation by the appropriate institutional or regional accrediting association as a requisite to specialized accrediting status. All of the agencies focus their standards on two common goals: identifying programs that meet agency standards and sustaining and enhancing a program's ability to prepare competent practitioners.

While there is considerable variety in the assessment methodologies of the accrediting process, the following features are predominate:

Institutional self-study with faculty involvement.

On-site evaluation by a team of professional peers and practitioners.

Definitions of specific procedures for conducting the study and collecting and reporting data.

Competency or performance-based assessments of professional practice, and evaluations of field or internship affiliations and experiences.

The prescriptive nature of the data collection and reporting requirements often extends to the institution's follow-up and annual reports.

Accreditation is one of many activities sponsored by professional organizations. Many have commissions or committees designated by their membership to carry out the accrediting purpose. For the senior professions, e.g., medicine, law, optometry, and library science, the function is an adjunct activity. Staff support is determined by the nature and makeup of the sponsoring organization. Prescriptive standards and guidelines reduce the need for staff consultation.

State Agencies

While the statutory powers, organizational structures, scope of authority, and approaches to evaluation vary considerably across state higher education agencies, the following features emerge:

New Program Approval

Statewide agencies or governing boards of most states are involved in some degree in new program review for public institutions. Several also conduct new program reviews of independent institutions.

Licensing or Certification

Programs leading to certification or licensing are reviewed by most states. Programs commonly covered include teacher preparation, nursing, architecture, engineering, and mortuary science.

Sharing Responsibilities

State level agencies frequently share responsibilities for comprehensive or program review. A number of state agencies have working agreements with regional or specialized accrediting agencies that permit representatives to have access to self-study reports and to accompany site-visit teams.

Recent Trends

Two noteworthy trends in the accrediting environment are cooperation between institutional and specialized agencies, and a growing emphasis on educational outcomes. Many colleges and universities undergo accrediting reviews by both institutional associations and one or more specialized agencies. Few have reached this condition as a result of a long-range or preconceived plan. The multiple accreditations of a given college or university are the products of internal and external pressures, professionalization, and competition for qualified students. As a consequence of this piecemeal development, an institution's constituencies may be perplexed and frustrated by the requirements, costs, and burdens imposed by multiple accreditations.

Recognizing the need for cooperation, the institutional, specialized, and state agencies respond by philosophically agreeing to the role, reach, and process of accreditation. Many consent to conduct the accreditation process using a common design. The design is (1) self-study, requiring the collection and analysis of data and the reporting of findings; (2) followed by an on-site visit by an evaluation team; and (3) review and action by the governing body of the agencies. They cooperate in scheduling the accrediting reviews and team visits. While reports are prepared by each accrediting unit, the crossover of institutional data, internal studies, and the liaisons between departments, divisions, and schools result in economies of time and effort.

This coordination realizes the full potential of the self-study process, the key tool of the accreditation process.

The second, more significant trend in the accrediting environment is the emphasis on educational outcomes measuring the college or university's success in achieving its objectives. The presumed purpose of every college and university is to produce certain results. The outcomes of an education are what the student learns and can do as a consequence of the education. The outcomes-oriented process features the translation of mission into clearly defined educational goals and objectives that are explicit enough to be assessed. It provides for a systematic and regular means of collecting, organizing, and analyzing performance data to determine whether the goals and objectives are being achieved, and the use of these assessments to maintain and improve educational effectiveness. In some states, outcomes data drive not only the review process, but the funding appropriations as well.

The centrality of assessment in the self-study process is underscored by its prominent place in the accrediting agencies' standards and criteria, and agency requirements for programs by which the institution documents its achievements. Factors that have prompted this focus include the national concern about higher education's accomplishments and the best selling voices of E. D. Hirsch's *Cultural Literacy: What Every American Needs to Know* and Allan Bloom's, *The Closing of the American Mind: How Higher Education Has Failed Democracy and Impoverished the Souls of Today's Students*. Each of the regional accrediting associations has developed documents to assist an institution in developing outcomes measurements and assessment processes, and conferences to help its members work with these documents.

Libraries and the Accrediting Associations

All of the regional associations and many of the specialized accrediting agencies have statements in their standards and policy documents regarding the academic library. Frequently cited topics include:

1. The library's importance as an academic resource.
2. The importance of mission, goals, and objectives in supporting the purposes of the library's constituencies.
3. The relationship of the library's resources and services to its parent institution's instructional and research goals and programs.
4. The quality (nature, scope, and size) of collections, staff, and physical facilities.

5. The availability of access services enabling the user to locate and use information not locally available.
6. Reference, library instruction, and referral assistance to enable the user to identify, select, and use information resources.
7. The nature and extent of collections and services.
8. The financial and organizational abilities to support the faculty and student needs.
9. The mechanisms used to communicate with constituents.

Accrediting agency statements support ongoing evaluation of the library's effectiveness. They identify data sources and advise that the academic library describe its plans and programs, and provide evidence of its strengths and weaknesses. Together with its parent institution, the library will identify a course of action supporting its strengths and addressing its needs.

None of the regional accrediting associations endorse or recommend the use of the Association of College and Research Libraries (ACRL) standards and guidelines, the Association of Research Libraries (ARL) documents, or other professional association documents. To advocate the standards of a professional organization would compromise the accrediting agencies' effectiveness in addressing their basic purposes: strengthening and sustaining the quality and integrity of the institution as a whole, and making it worthy of public confidence. However, there are common threads among the regional association standards and those of academic libraries. For example, the following excerpts from ACRL standards are similar to statements in accrediting agency documents:

> The College shall develop a comprehensive statement of the mission of the learning resources program based on the nature and purpose of the institution.
>
> *Standards for Community, Junior and Technical College*
> *Learning Resources Programs (1990) Standard 1.0*

> The library shall maintain a systematic and continuous program for evaluating its performance, for informing the community of its accomplishments, and for identifying needed improvements.
>
> *College Library Standards (1986) Standard 7.4.1*

> The mission of the university library is to provide information services in support of the teaching, research, and public service missions of the university. The achievement of that mission requires the development of standards to address the ways in which goals should be developed and measured, needed resources estimated, and success in goal achievement evaluated.
>
> *Standards for University Libraries (1989) General Statement of Purpose*

While the accrediting process provides a framework for referencing ACRL standards in the institutional self-study, the accrediting associations do not employ them in their assessments or decisions. Likewise, the specialized accrediting agencies covering professional disciplines or schools require the academic library to respond to criteria, guidelines, and processes that are often more sharply focused than those employed in institution-wide accreditation. The library's response may be prescribed and directed. It may be required to report specific data (e.g., collection size, subject fields, expenditures, staff allocations), evidence of use of resources and services, and rankings of the professional program's collection and support. The process often uses questionnaires and prescribed formats and is less open to the individual library's development and interpretation. The library's ongoing relationship with the program will define its opportunities to interpret the format and enhance its contribution.

The recent trend of accrediting bodies to employ the educational outcomes concept and assessments of student achievement accommodates several recent developments in academic librarianship. A number of academic libraries are employing outcomes that lend themselves to evaluation. By means of library use, user satisfaction, materials use, and materials access measures and document delivery, and reference transaction records, these libraries make informed decisions about programs and resource allocation. They rely on the understanding and application of the collected data and the extent to which the library is realizing its objectives. The use of these measures in accrediting self-study reports will lend credibility to the library's role and its contribution to the institution.

The accrediting environment for most academic institutions is one of change involving multiple reporting and review agencies and accountability issues. The academic library must prepare to respond to this environment by regularly monitoring:

1. The accrediting associations and agencies covering the institution.
2. The criteria and procedures prescribed for the institution and the library.
3. The schedules for review and accreditation.
4. The institution's liaison officer with the association or agency.
5. The library's record with the association or agency, including ongoing or outstanding concerns regarding library matters and the library's responses to those concerns.

An Inventory of Accrediting Associations and Agencies, a sample document for maintaining a record of this information, is shown in Figure 1.1.

Additional Readings

"Assessing Student Academic Achievement." *NCA Quarterly* 66, no. 2 (Fall 1991): entire issue.

Astin, Alexander W. *Assessment for Excellence.* New York: Macmillan, 1991.

Bloom, Allan D. *The Closing of the American Mind.* New York: Simon and Schuster, 1987.

Casserly, Mary. "Academic Library Regional Accreditation." *College and Research Libraries* 47 (January 1986): 38–47.

Council on Postsecondary Accreditation. *Glossary.* Washington, D.C.: Council on Postsecondary Accreditation, April 1982. Reported to the COPA Board, April 12–16, 1982 as a document that "may be used by those who wish but will not be published (by COPA)."

Harris, Sherry S., ed. *Accredited Institutions of Postsecondary Education, 90–91.* Washington, D. C. Published for the Council on Postsecondary Accreditation by American Council on Education, 1991 (or most recent edition).

Hirsch, Eric D. *Cultural Literacy: What Every American Needs to Know.* Boston: Houghton Mifflin, 1987.

Kania, Antoinette M. "Academic Library Standards and Performance Measures." *College and Research Libraries* 49 (January 1988): 16–23.

Kania-Schicchi, Antoinette. "The Development of a Model Set of Regional Accreditation Standards for Academic Libraries." Ph.D. diss., Rutgers University, 1984.

Kells, H. R. *Self-Study Processes.* 3rd ed. New York: American Council on Education and Macmillan Publishing Company, 1988.

Neal, M. T., H. R. Kells and Laura J. Kells. *Bibliography on Postsecondary Accreditation.* Washington, D. C.: Council on Postsecondary Accreditation, 1984.

Pascarella, E.T. and P.T. Terenzini. *How College Affects Students.* San Francisco: Jossey-Bass, 1991.

Sellen, Mary. "Specialized Accreditation and the Library." *Collection Building* 11, no. 3 (1991): 2–8.

"Standards for College Libraries, 1986." *C&RL News* 47 (March 1986): 189–200.

"Standards for Community, Junior and Technical College Learning Resources Programs." *C&RL News* 51 (Sept. 1990): 757–67.

"Standards for University Libraries." *C&RL News* 50 (September 1989): 679–91.

Thrash, Patricia A. "A Report on the Role of Outcomes Evaluation in the Accreditation Process." *NCA Quarterly* 65 (Fall 1990): 481–90.

Virgo, Julie Carroll and David Alan Yuro, eds. *Libraries and Accreditation in Institutions of Higher Education.* Proceedings of a Conference held in New York City, June 26–27, 1980. Chicago: Association of College and Research Libraries, 1981.

Young, Kenneth E., Charles M. Chambers, H. R. Kells, and Associates. *Understanding Accreditation.* San Francisco: Jossey-Bass, 1983.

FIGURE 1.1 Inventory of Accrediting Associations and Agencies: Our Academic Library

Agency	Program coverage	Institution liaison officer	Agency documents/library references	Date of next review	Related documents of last review
Middle States	Comprehensive	Provost	*Characteristics of Excellence in Higher Education.* Rev. 1991 pp. 34–36	1998	Our Library Self-Study 1992 Our University Special Topics Self-Study 1993 MSA Team Evaluation Report April 1993 Our Library's Action Plan 1993–97
National Council for Accreditation of Teacher Education	Education; Programs for Preparation of Teachers	Dean of the School of Education	NCATE. *Standards, Procedures, and Policies for the Accreditation of Professional Education Units.* 1990 pp. 58–59	1995	Our University Report to NCATE 1990 NCATE Team Report October 1990
National League of Nursing	Nursing	Nursing Department Chair	*Criteria for the Evaluation of BA and Higher Degree Programs in Nursing.* 1992 *Policies and Procedures of Accreditation for Programs in Nursing Education.* 6th ed. 1990 *Educational Outcomes: Assessment of Quality. Compendium of Measurement Tools for Baccalaureate Nursing Programs.* 1988		Our University NLN Self-Study Report 1992 National League of Nursing Council Action Report. November 1992 Our Library's Collection Development Program. 1990–

Chapter Two Accreditation Practices and Procedures

The impetus for the review of the institution and its programs comes from the accrediting agency. The library needs to understand the accrediting agency's focus and its parent institution's plans for responding to the agency before developing its review or completing the report forms. This chapter outlines the tasks associated with an accreditation review and describes the interlinking roles of the agency, the institution, and the library in the accrediting process. Figure 2.1 is based on the accreditation process that employs the self-study model. It identifies the common tasks associated with the process and who carries them out.

The Agency Role

The accrediting agency notifies its member institution of a forthcoming review and its timetable. Along with the schedule, the agency provides the institution with documents that describe the agency's procedures and expectations and identifies the staff who will interpret the criteria or advise on preparations for the review. These documents typically include standards or statements of criteria defining the conditions required for accreditation, self-study design models, descriptions of procedures, and data collection requirements or forms. The typical self-study designs are (1) a comprehensive model, which supports the examination of the entire institutional program; (2) a comprehensive/special emphasis model, which is holistic but examines particular programs or processes in greater depth; (3) a strategic planning program, which supports the institution's development and implementation of a planning model based on mission, purposes, and resources; or (4) a special topics model in which the review is focused on an in-depth analysis of selected functions, issues, or programs, but includes a comprehensive overview component.

In addition to informing its members of the self-study models and advising them on the selection, most of the institutional associations provide training workshops for faculty and staff members about to embark on an accreditation review. Workshop topics cover self-study design, data collection and analysis, outcomes assessments, and agency expectations. Case study exercises enable the participants to acquire a knowledge of the agency's requirements, to engage in communication processes, and to practice problem-solving techniques. Agency personnel who conduct these workshops are also available as consultants to accreditation participants throughout the review process.

The accrediting agency is responsible for selecting and training the visiting peer evaluation team. It conducts workshops to train peer reviewers and provides team members with manuals on the peer review process and procedures. Peer reviewers are responsible for studying the institution's self-study report, visiting the campus, meeting with appropriate campus representatives, and assessing the institution's quality and integrity. They prepare an evaluation report that is usually discussed with campus representatives. The visiting team reports its findings to the board of the accrediting agency together with a recommendation on accreditation action.

In formulating its accreditation decision the accrediting agency's board or accreditation committee review: (1) the institution's reports and self-study documents, (2) the peer evaluation team's reports and recommendations, (3) the institution's response to the evaluation team's report, and (4) discussions with the peer evaluation team chair and agency staff.

Accreditation actions are usually in one of the following categories:

1. Initial accreditation without or with a request for follow-up reports and/or visits within a specified period of time. The re-evaluation calendar is usually shorter than the one following a reaffirmation decision.
2. Reaffirmation of accreditation without condition, or with requests for follow-up letters, reports, or visits on an identified schedule.
3. Deferment of a decision to permit an institution to correct serious weaknesses and report specific information to the agency on an established schedule.
4. Show cause order requiring an institution to present its case by means of a substantive report and on-site evaluation visits. If the institution is unable to meet the agency's requirements, it is denied accreditation or removed from the list of the agency's accredited institutions.
5. The denial of accreditation to a candidate institution applying for initial accreditation. The institution may be permitted to

continue candidate status until it undergoes a reevaluation within a specified period of time.

Accompanying all accreditation or reaccreditation actions are requirements for periodic review reports providing the agency with an overview of the institution or its specialized program, and responding to the report of the last evaluation. Some agencies collect input data on enrollments, instructional resources, and finances while others require descriptions of specific conditions or program quality assessments.

Librarians and the Agency Role

To understand the agency's role in the accreditation process, the library staff is advised to:

1. Identify and obtain the accrediting agency's standards and procedures documents.
2. Read agency documents that describe its processes and expectations and its newsletters and journals.
3. Attend accrediting agency–sponsored workshops and seminars preparing participants for accrediting and reaccrediting reviews and activities.
4. Seek opportunities to become an intern or member of the agency's visiting peer evaluation teams. The additional training team members receive is applicable to program assessment tasks in general, and the experience of visiting and evaluating other institutions provides valuable perspectives to accreditation preparation.

A primary objective of these activities is to acquire a comprehensive knowledge of the accrediting agency's purposes and processes. This perspective will enhance the library's ability to identify its role and reporting requirements and strengthen its contributions at the institutional level. The library sections of the accrediting agency documents must be studied carefully too, but an understanding of them depends on knowledge of the complete documents and the accrediting agency's modus operandi.

The Parent Institution's Role

When an institution is notified by the accrediting agency of an upcoming review, it works with the agency to prepare for the review. The extent of the planning is dictated by the objectives of the review and the resources applied to it. Many of the elements of the accrediting review are established during the initial assessment and design phases in consultation with the accrediting agency. The consensus developed in this consultation is the basis for the "go ahead" and the accrediting agency's approval of the self-study design.

Preparing for the accrediting review is a series of steps beginning with the clarification of the purposes of the accrediting review and advancing to the results and their applications. Along the way the participation of the institution's constituencies—its students, faculty, staff, alumni, and trustees—is an essential component. The self-study model described in Figure 2.1 summarizes these steps. This planning phase has these goals:

Defining the Purposes of the Accrediting Review and Boundaries

In setting the stage for the review, the institution's plan identifies the accrediting review's objectives and goals and the institution's self-study design or requirements for responding to the agency's format. Boundaries to be considered are time, financial resources, and work-load limitations. All costs should be considered in light of available resources and sufficient funding allocated to support the accrediting review. A master schedule is developed to support the review, acknowledging the institution's academic calendar and other related events, and the agency's reporting requirements.

Defining Appropriate Work Groups and Providing a Clear Mandate for Each

Tasks for this phase include developing an overall accrediting review plan including the approaches to be used and the tactics for gathering information. Because the design of most accrediting reviews follows from a statement of mission and goals, updating and/or clarifying these statements are frequent points of departure. The self-study design is the framework guiding the formations of the working groups and the definition of their tasks. The charge for each group clearly defines its assignment, calendar, and the style and format for working drafts and final reports.

Choosing the Participants and Identifying Their Responsibilities

At the institutional level, a planning or steering committee usually manages the accrediting review. This group identifies the review's dimensions, provides orientation for the group members, sets and monitors the schedule, arranges for review of drafts and final reports, and oversees the preparation of the document to be reviewed by the accrediting agency. Appointments include the chairpersons of the steering committee and study topic groups. The leadership of individuals who have high credibility and serve as opinion leaders of the constituencies they represent can be critical. So too is the careful selection of persons who will focus on the requirements of the review and work together to accomplish them. The members of the planning and study groups will possess skills to define and clarify problems and conduct and participate in effective meetings.

Preparing for Audience Involvement

The accreditation review will touch the lives of many people in the institution. Their *involvement* includes the early, active participation of students, faculty, trustees, administrators, and alumni who will be affected by, or responsible for, the results. The campus climate can be strongly affected by this audience's understanding of the review's purposes. Communication plans—who will receive what information and when they will obtain it—should be agreed upon at this early stage. This will support audience involvement and establish credibility of the accrediting review's findings.

Guiding and Supporting the On-going Activities of the Review

The level of effort required to support these activities is often related to the amount of information the work groups decide to gather and analyze, and the sources of the information. An institution generally has a significant amount of diverse, useful data on the campus. The collection, and preparation of the data and information, and its analysis and interpretation are complex tasks. If special tools or instruments are employed to yield findings for the accrediting review, the activity carries many implications for personnel resources. Personnel with special expertise in the area of research and evaluation are required. The use of a broadly based data collection and analysis team is a means for coordinating and integrating data collection efforts and interpreting and communicating the findings.

An important task in this phase is supporting the development of fair and complete written reports. Including multiple perspectives within and between the accrediting review's groups addresses the need for balanced reporting of strengths and weaknesses and safeguards against distortion by personal feelings and biases.

Communicating with the Review's Participants and the Institution's
Constituencies to Obtain Their Insights and Understandings

The planning committee presents the results to the institution's constituents and allows for an adequate period of time for discussion, the
exploration of unexpected findings, and textual revisions. With the
press of time this often takes place with the first draft of a self-study
report. Including faculty, students, staff, trustees, and alumni representatives in this review is imperative as the success of this phase, the
utilization of the feedback, is dependent upon receiving informed
observations and opinions. Those constituents need access to this
draft for review and study.

Reporting the Results of the Review

Preparing a useful report is a matter of recognizing the criteria and
standards of the accrediting agency within the context of the goals,
achievements, and plans of the institution. The process requires selecting data, presenting clear and well-organized analyses of findings
and recommendations, and writing an organized, coherent report.
The report for a comprehensive type self-study often covers the institution's examination and analysis of these areas:

1. The institution's mission, goals, and objectives.
2. The curriculum and the teaching and learning processes.
3. Programs for assessing student academic achievement, and the
   degree to which these programs contribute to teaching and
   learning improvements.
4. Recruitment and enrollment policies, efforts, and results.
5. Student services, e.g., advising, counseling, health, athletic,
   social, and other cocurricular activities, and student-faculty-
   administrative relations.
6. The role of the faculty in providing instruction and participating in the formation of educational policies and programs and
   institutional governance.
7. The organization for facilitating the attainment of the institution's goals and objectives.
8. The governing board's role in ensuring the fulfillment of its
   announced mission and goals.
9. Planning and resource allocation policies and practices.
10. The roles of the library, computing, and other learning re-
    sources in meeting instructional objectives.
11. The adequacy of its plant and equipment.
12. Its catalog, publications, and general public relations goals and
    practices.

13. Its openness to innovation, experimentation, and future growth.

The self-study report is an analysis of the parent institution's programs and their consistency or variance with the institution's mission, goals, and objectives. The report identifies the human, physical, and fiscal resources the institution is employing to achieve its aims, and it forecasts their future availability.

Preparing the Institution for Change

The concluding step in the review project is preparing for change. The review process generates recommendations for change, and creates a climate for these results. Changes in institutions require a complex set of conditions, including motivation for change, and an understanding of needs. The conditions for facilitating the use of the accrediting review recommendations are fostered within the review process itself. The value of the self-study and reporting documents is in their abilities to signal the need for change and provide the substance for planning, program reviews, and action agendas. While it is unlikely that the institution will adopt a plan or reviewing system that mirrors the accreditation report, the selective use of the self-study's features, including peer perspective, yields results and supports the change process. The collective experience of the self-study process—building shared vision and team learning and clarifying realities—positions the institution for change.

Library Participation at the Institutional Level

Ideally, the library not only becomes knowledgeable about the accrediting agency's requirements, but participates in its institution's plans for the accrediting review. To become a well-informed active voice, the library is advised to:

1. Assume a leadership role on campus. Many librarians are experienced in appraising organizational performance, preparing reports, and implementing action agendas. The library sees the process as a means of articulating the institution's purpose and is able to address the requirements of an institution-level process. It should capitalize on these abilities.

2. Seek an appointment to the institution's planning/steering committee which presides over review processes. The composition of this group may depend on tradition, position responsibilities, and the political realities of the institution. The library is directly affected by

the process and seeks this opportunity to contribute to institution-wide planning and decision making.

3. Use the institution-wide process to facilitate the library's communication with its community. Activities such as participating in institutional problem-solving activities and developing strategies for institutional change will increase the visibility of the library and strengthen the institution's commitment to the library goals.

Although each institution selects the planning or steering committee members in a manner that reflects its unique governance process and particular staff resources, the appointing officer wants an able group of representative persons who can work together to accomplish the self-study task. It is essential that this group provide the review with knowledgeable and critical perspectives focused on the accrediting review's purposes. Although no single criteria apply in matters of steering committee compositions, and the matter is always situational, the selection criteria often identify persons with these qualities:

Credibility: objectivity, trustworthiness, and an orientation to the good of the institution.

Interest: past history of involvement in similar efforts and an openness to new perspectives and program ideas.

Available time: past record of responsible time management.

Expertise: experience in curriculum and program development, knowledge of current trends in higher education, ability to identify information needed and to collect, analyze, and report this information.

Communication skills: adeptness at interviewing and listening, speaking and writing clearly, and managing bias and conflict.

For many institutions the most important criteria are a track record of time management and the ability to identify, collect, analyze, and report information. Strong institution-wide knowledge, interest, and an enthusiasm for the study are often the elements that will shape it. In these areas the academic librarian is likely to be exceptionally qualified for steering committee or other self-study group membership.

Library Participation at the Library Level

Given the knowledge of the accrediting agency's criteria and purposes and its parent institution's plan, the library's next step is to identify the essential elements to be included in a review of the library. No list of essential elements can be all inclusive, since every review is different in purpose and scope. Topics that might be covered in one situation might not be included in another. Flexibility and adaptability are important. So too are the roles of the library staff transcending the parochially defined boundries, supporting user's needs, and equitable and efficient ways of utilizing library resources and services.

Development of the review plan requires a concerted effort at the beginning of the review. Once the elements are agreed upon and personnel assignments are in place, the progress of the review is routinely monitored and adjustments are readily made to accommodate changing circumstances. The individual elements of the library's plan are discussed in more detail in the following sections.

Accreditation Project Management

The best way to ensure adequate preparation is to assign a library staff member with these qualifications to the responsibility of coordinating accreditation activities. This accreditation project manager will be a person who:

1. Occupies a position that is regularly involved in library planning and evaluation, and in discussions concerning policies, procedures, and data collection.
2. Is skilled in planning and managing a project, conducting effective meetings, and facilitating group processes.
3. Can expand the effort through presentations and participating in bringing about the changes resulting from the library groups' findings.
4. Is comfortable with and skilled at report writing, data analysis, and long-term projects.
5. Interacts well with faculty, administrators, and members of policy-setting and governing groups.

The accreditation project manager is often the library director. If not, the manager must be the choice of the library director. There is a need for a good set of understandings between the director and the project manager concerning their roles and what steps the director will participate in, and when the director will be consulted about the project's work. The project manager is a person who exercises good judgment, commands respect for the library, and has the abilities to interface the library with all aspects and schedules of the accreditation process. The project manager's responsibilities include:

1. Keeping abreast of the general literature involving accreditation, in particular the standards of the applicable accreditation associations and the library professions.
2. Creating and maintaining channels that will enable the library's study group members to actively participate and do their work.
3. Participating as a full-fledged member of the study group, such as attending meetings, carrying out assignments, and generally sharing the work load.
4. Maintaining staff awareness of accreditation processes, procedures, and requirements.
5. Monitoring and interfacing with the college's plans and schedules for accreditation visits.
6. Serving as the initial library contact for the college's accrediting teams, committees, and study groups, although other library staff members may be assigned as well.
7. Insuring that data collection and special reporting activities are conducted on schedules that are timely and appropriate for the accreditation visit and supportive of the library's operations and service commitments.
8. Bringing standards and accreditation requirements to bear in discussions of library policies and procedures, including data collection and reports.
9. Coordinating the library's report writing and data presentation in the accreditation report.
10. Overseeing the library's response to recommendations regarding the library as a result of the accreditation visit.

The project manager has provisions made in advance for the time to address these responsibilities and support for dispatching paperwork, collecting data, and preparing reports.

Some institutions, at the institutional or library level, appoint a committee, task force, or study group to address the library component of the accrediting review. In this environment, a group of five or six is usually adequate to provide the necessary participation and expertise. If the chair is not the library's project manager, the chair will work closely with the project manager who will be the library's chief liaison with the committee. The chair of the group sets the tone and pace of the group's work and should be someone in rapport with the library director and project manager. The chair needs good communication skills, gifts of library advocacy, and the abilities to lead the group and keep it on schedule.

In small institutions or some specialized accrediting reviews, much of the work in conducting the study and preparing the report will be accomplished by the library director. This alternative to a study group structure is efficient and can produce an analytical and perceptive report. A key to its usefulness continues to be the active participation of user constituents and the library staff in bringing together findings and articulating recommendations. The successful employment of the report in the library's planning processes is reinforced by this interaction.

When a group is the means for addressing the library component of the accrediting review, it is important that this committee or task force be prepared to do its work. With a skilled chair and carefully selected membership, the place to start is the written charge which sets forth the institution's expectations for the library's review and the committee's role in addressing them. The preparation of the charge should involve the library director or project manager. The charge should include:

- The tasks and role of the group in the library's review.
- The scope and limits of its role.
- Key issues or questions the group is expected to address.
- A description of the accrediting agency's criteria, guidelines, or directives to be addressed.
- References to accrediting documents applicable to the group's tasks.
- A definition of the consultation and reporting requirements with institutional-level committees, the library director, and institutional officers.
- Instruction as to the form of the group's report.

The group will also define its supporting requirements for funding, staff assistance, and communication protocols (what, how, and with whom). Whether the accrediting review is guided by the library's accreditation project manager or a committee/task force, getting the job done requires preparing a plan for accomplishing its objectives. The elements in the planning process are planning, scheduling, budgeting, and reporting.

Planning

The starting point is a planning process that enables the group to discuss their purposes and become oriented to the accrediting agency's requirements. To get underway, the participants set working schedules and target dates for completing key tasks and identify budgetary resources, staff support, and resource persons who can be consulted as the self-study unfolds. They acquaint themselves with applicable accrediting agency policies and procedures, their institution's plan for the conduct of their work, and what topics or problems to study. The project manager or chair provides each participant with copies of relevant guidelines and arranges briefings, as appropriate, by the parent institution's steering committee. The participants will be permitted to clarify their assignment until they know what is expected of them.

The result of these discussions is a planning document described here as a work plan (see figure 2.2 for the definition of activities covering one of the tasks). Every review should have a work plan, even a simple one, because it specifies the path by which the review will be accomplished. The work plan answers these questions:

- What will be studied and reviewed? Why?
- What evidence and data will be collected? How is each suited to its purpose?
- What analysis and interpretation is needed?
- Is the study to conclude with recommendations, appropriate solutions, and/or plans?
- What reports will be prepared? In what formats?
- Who will accomplish these tasks?
- When will the library director, the steering committee and other administrative officers and constituents be contacted, participate in, or be consulted about the process, analyses, and findings?
- What condition/activity indicates that the group's work is completed?
- Will the participants participate in a review of their findings? Take action on their recommendations or related derivatives?

The work plan should contain the following information:

- The listing of the tasks.
- The description of each task and the activities within each task that will be done.
- The sequence, in chronological order, of each activity in the task.
- The names of persons responsible for seeing that each task is accomplished.

- The names of persons who will participate in carrying out the task, those to be consulted, and those to be contacted and informed of progress and results.
- A description of "what" completes a task.
- The starting and due dates for each task.
- The reporting form for findings and recommendations.

The work plan may also list key documents, e.g., accrediting agency criteria and standards, the institution's accrediting review plan, mission and goal statements, and data sources. The work plan's schedule sequences the tasks on a common, institution-wide schedule. For a simple review, the timetable may be a listing of due dates matched with each task. The work plan can be a grid-type document that can be easily absorbed by the library staff and the institutional level steering committee in a few minutes. Its most significant contributions are the exercise of thinking through the accreditation project and initiating preparations for getting the job done. Important too is its recognition of constraints, time limitations, staff shortages, and current service obligations, that set parameters for the scope of the review.

Budgets

Inherent in any accrediting review process are financial and office resources to support the review. Any review incurs predictable costs for staff support and the production and distribution of reports. Some reviews involve hard to predict costs for the selection, use, and interpretive analysis of evaluative instruments. If there is a limit to expenditures or constraints under which the participants must work, such as the amount of time per week they can spend on the review, it needs to be acknowledged to allow them to plan realistically and avoid disappointment.

The library participants need to know the financial supporting requirements and the plans for its use. A budget and staff support plan may be prepared at the institutional planning level with a library interface. The simplest budgeting methodology for the library is to use its work plan and identify costs that are those of the accrediting review. If funds have been allocated for the library's study or if there are limits to expenditures, the library must work within those conditions. The library's participation at the institutional level is key to obtaining budget support.

Staff support is vital to the library's review. An ideal arrangement is for data input and analysis, and recordkeeping and reporting requirements to be scheduled in hours and by calendar days, and for the support to be included in staffing schedules. Office support of a microcomputer for participant and secretarial use, e.g., microcomputer support with wordprocessing and spreadsheet software, is essential. The library's management information system—the data it routinely collects and analyzes to measure and report its performance—will be a key contributor to the accrediting review. Its sophistication may significantly reduce the time spent on data-based tasks.

Data Collection and Analysis

Collecting data which is meaningful to the accrediting review is critical to the success of the process. Too many efforts are flawed or useless when the data collected tells the library nothing about the problem or how to solve it, when its analysis is flawed by faulty assumptions, and when it is inconsistent and unreliable. It is easy to become lost in a sea of useless data and to spend an inordinate amount of time on the wrong course.

Data collection requirements are defined by these questions:

- Why are we collecting data?
- What data will be collected?
- How will the data help us address the purposes of the accrediting review?
- What are we trying to evaluate?
- What is the plan for collecting the data? What procedures will be used?
- Who will record it?
- What is the plan for analyzing the results? What goals—user expectations—will be used in the analysis? Who will conduct the analysis?
- What are the reporting schedules?

The collection and analysis of data will employ the best measures the library has to identify its performance and its problems as called for by the accrediting review. During the course it may need to resolve issues concerning problem identification, the library users' needs, methods of measurement, and interpretation. In the final analysis, the library will look to the data for causes and conclusions, and the setting of action agendas. The crux of the data collection and analysis activity is to enable the library to diagnose and know its current conditions. If it has not achieved reliability and stability in its performance measures activity, these data tasks may help it do so and come closer to responding to its constituents' needs.

The format is an important aspect of reporting the data collection analysis and findings. Reports should describe outcomes and data collection studies, show findings, and use easy-to-read charts to display them. They should forecast the impact, describe the implications of the findings, and conclude with a summary statement that repeats the essentials. Librarians searching for ways to present quantitative information effectively will find Edward Tufte's *The Visual Display of Quantitative Information* a useful reference.

Reporting

The library's report is often a three-stage process involving the composition of a draft report or reporting forms, acknowledging the responses of the institution's constituents to the draft, and fitting the report into the institutional level report. The form of the library's report may be defined by the accrediting agency or the planning committee of the parent institution. For some specialized accrediting agencies, the report may consist of completed forms and/or written responses to questionnaires. When the reporting formats do not call for goal achievement information, the library may elect to append this information in a clearly written document that relates to the agency's standards.

The preparation of a useful report is not an easy task. Too often these reports are long on description and short on analysis, identification of outcomes, and recommendations for sustaining performance levels or accomplishing changes. The "desired attributes" of a self-study report defined by Kells (pp.131–132) are that the report is:

1. Clearly written and well organized.
2. Concise.
3. Focused on key issues.
4. Frank and balanced view of the (library's) program.
5. Useful for several audiences—boards, potential donors, state agencies, staff members, student and community leaders, and one or more accrediting agencies.
6. Systematic in its references to how the standards of the agency are met.

Figure 2.3 presents a sample table of contents for a library self-study report.

While the accrediting agency is an audience in the reporting process, the library's constituents are primary. Given the findings of its review, the library may report at these or other stages:

When it has documented a problem and looks for user input.

When it has documented the cause of a problem and proposes a solution.

At the conclusion of the self-study.

At whatever stage, the library's report should be focused on the objectives of the accrediting review, covering its context (specific or comprehensive) and purpose. It will share key activities and results in ways that are understandable to its constituents. In the course of developing a report—in part or in whole—the library is advised to "test it out" on a sample audience such as the library committee. An outline for the report follows:

I. Executive Summary

  The purpose of the accrediting review
  Major findings
  Recommendations/next steps

II. Description of the review/self-study

  Conditions reviewed
  Data collection and analysis activities. In summary, avoid detailed descriptions.
  Findings
  Recommendations. Describe potential improvements.

III. Conclusions

  Impact of findings on the library
  Suggestions for future work
  Suggestions for the library staff
  Other recommendations
  Acknowledgments

Usually experienced with written reports, the library may be less so with oral presentations. Oral presentations should not take more than 30 minutes (or less as defined by the circumstances) and involve, whenever possible, each study group member in the presentation. Repeating the major findings and the related recommendations will help the audience understand the substance of the report. Both written and oral reports should invite students, faculty, and staff to respond to the findings. An oral report is a special opportunity to listen, build consensus, and discuss improvements. Do the results address our needs? Do you agree with the conclusions? Do you advise something else?

Additional Readings

Beck, William L. and Marsha L. Nolf. "The Process and Value of Self-Study in a Medium-sized University Library." *College and Research Libraries* 53 (March 1992): 150–62.

Bergquist, W. H. and Armstrong, J. R. *Planning Effectively for Educational Quality: An Outcomes Based Approach for Colleges Committed to Excellence.* San Francisco: Jossey-Bass, 1986.

Ewell, Peter T. and Robert P. Lisensky. *Assessing Institutional Effectiveness: Redirecting the Self-Study Process.* Washington, D.C.: Consortium for the Advancement of Private Higher Education, 1988.

Fordyce, Jack K. and Raymond Weil. *Managing with People.* 2nd ed. Reading, Mass.: Addison-Wesley, 1978.

Gardner, Jeffrey J. *Strategic Plans in ARL Libraries.* SPEC Kit 158. Washington, D.C.: Association of Research Libraries, 1989.

Kania, Antoinette M. "Self-Study Methods for the Library and the LRC." *New Directions for Community Colleges* no. 71 (Fall 1990): 81–90.

Kells, H. R. *Self-Study Process.* 3rd ed. New York: American Council on Education and Macmillan, 1988.

"Tips for Librarians Planning for Accreditation Visits." *C&RL News* 53 (July/August 1992): 447.

Tufte, Edward R. *The Visual Display of Quantitative Information.* Cheshire, Conn.: Graphics Press, 1983.

FIGURE 2.1   An Outline of Accreditation Tasks: Self-Study Model

Tasks	Responsibility
Notifying institution of forthcoming review and its schedules	Accrediting Agency
Reviewing and evaluating self-study design options	Accrediting Agency and Parent Institution
Selecting self-study design	Parent Institution

Organizing the self-study process
  Selecting and appointing leaders
  Defining tasks and assignments
  Obtaining supporting resources
  Establishing participant work groups
  Setting and publishing a master calendar describing key events and due dates
  Designing and implementing a communication delivery system that supports discussion and feedback
	Parent Institution

Conducting the self-study
  Reviewing accrediting agency standards
  Clarifying mission and goals and identifying related programs and activities
  Selecting instruments to collect and analyze information
  Collecting and analyzing information
  Compiling findings
  Composing a draft self-study report
  Sharing the draft in open forums involving the institution's students, faculty, trustees, and alumni constituents; and reviewing the responses for self-study contributions
  Amending and editing the self-study report
	Parent Institution

Publishing and distributing the self-study report	Parent Institution
Preparing for the visit of the accrediting team	Parent Institution and Accrediting Agency

FIGURE 2.1 (Continued)

Tasks	Responsibility
Hosting the accrediting teams on-site visit	Parent Institution
Making an on-site assessment and preparing a draft evaluation report	Accrediting Agency
Receiving the team's draft evaluation report and responding to its factual and interpretive contents	Parent Institution

Given the accrediting agency's action, preparing for:
    Ongoing program review
    Follow-up reports or visits
    Deferment responses (to allow an institution to correct serious weaknesses)
    Show cause responses (requiring a substantive report and on-site evaluation)
	Parent Institution

Linking the results of the self-study and the evaluation report to the institution's ongoing planning and budgeting processes	Parent Institution and Library

FIGURE 2.2   Our College Library Accrediting Agency Review:
             Work Plan and Schedule

Library's Report Due: 1-1-91

Project Manager: Director of Libraries

Library Unit: Director's Office

III.   Project Title: Obtain an overall view of student perceptions of the
           major strengths and weaknesses of the library.

Task No.	Task Description	Responsible Person	Hours	Date Due
1.	Review and evaluate existing information	Info. Services Librarian	4	9-16-90
2.	Determine if new information is needed	Info. Services Librarian	4	9-23-90
3.	Procure or design a data collection instrument for collecting the information	Info. Services Librarian	40	10-14-90
4.	Arrange tabulation services	Info. Services Librarian	8	10-20-90
5.	Pilot test the data collection instrument	Info. Services Librarian	8	10-20-90
6.	Employ the instrument	Info. Services Librarian	40	11-4-90
7.	Tabulate results	Secretary	10	11-11-90
8.	Analyze tabulations	Info. Services Librarian	20	11-18-90
9.	Draft report of findings	Info. Services Librarian	10	11-25-90
10.	Review report with project manager	Info. Services Librarian Director	2	12-10-90
11.	Amend report after review	Info. Services Librarian Staff Writer	2	12-12-90
12.	Submit report to project manager	Info. Services Librarian		12-15-90

FIGURE 2.3   Our College Library Self-Study Report
                    Comprehensive Type

Table of Contents

Chapter Three   Preparing for the Accreditation Review

The best way for libraries to prepare for the accreditation of their parent institution or any of its programs is to view accreditation not as an event, but as a process conducted on a cyclical basis. Accreditation activities culminate in a report that is a component of an ongoing self-study process. Preparation for accreditation should be conducted continually as part of the library's routine planning, reporting, and evaluating procedures. For the library the focus of that ongoing process is on its users—the people whom the library serves. Since library services are provided for people to use, two relationships become important. How does the provision of library services affect users and what they do? Are there tasks and work habits of users that affect, or should affect, the library? The accreditation visit is an occasion to share the responses to these questions, and user aspirations, staff observations, and self-study findings with peers external to the institution. The library should draw attention to its significant achievements, improvement opportunities, and its assessment processes—the evidence it has that it is addressing the needs of its users.

These interwoven elements form the nucleus of the library's management and self-evaluation processes and, not coincidentally, are the key elements under analysis in the accreditation process:

1. The library's statement of its mission, goals, and objectives.
2. User studies based on the needs, wants, and capabilities of students, faculty, and researchers evaluating the effectiveness of library services, programs, and policies.
3. Routinely collected data that reflects the success with which the library is meeting its objectives. This data should be presented so that it reflects recent internal trends. It may be amplified by comparative studies defining position with related standards, national norms, or ranking among cohort or competitive institutions.

4. Summative interpretive reports that assess progress in meeting goals and objectives.
5. Consultative processes achieving effective communication, review and analysis of options, and development of consensus regarding the library's goals and programs.

In the three sections of this chapter that follow, each of these elements and their key ingredients are described. The techniques for bringing them about are not an objective of this handbook, yet the approach relies heavily on the library's mission statement and its identification of goals. So too does it rely on an understanding and application of data.

SECTION I: Mission, Goals, and Objectives

The initial focal point of the library's self-study and accreditation processes is its statement of mission, goals, and objectives. The mission statement briefly defines the basic purpose and philosophy of the library as it relates to the mission of its parent institution and its community. It asserts the basic role and values of the library in relationship to its clientele. The goals tell how the library will accomplish its mission. They describe the functions of the library, its intended inputs, processes, and outcomes. The objectives make explicit the library's plans and strategies for achieving its goals within defined schedules and performance specifications.

The Mission Statement

The mission statement is a brief description of the purpose and philosophy of the library that identifies the clientele being served. The mission statement may be drafted by the library staff, reviewed with students and faculty, and approved by the parent institution's executive body responsible for acting on basic academic policy statements. The mission statement may be revised in accordance with the review schedule of the institution's mission statement, or at least every five years. Published and made available to students and faculty, it includes:

1. Identification of the parent institution and its students, faculty, and other constituent populations.
2. A statement of the fundamental purpose of the library.
3. An expression of the fundamental philosophy of the library.

4. Documented consistency with the mission of the institution.
5. Date of adoption and identification of the appropriate bodies reviewing and approving the statement.

Figure 3.1 is a worksheet to assist the development of the library mission statement. Figure 3.2 is a sample library mission statement presented as it might appear in a library accreditation report.

Goals

Goals are statements that express the basic functions of the library in terms of inputs (the resources and services it aims to provide), outputs (the achievements it aims to promote), and processes (the management methods and values it aims to employ). Goals are drafted by the library staff, reviewed with appropriate students and faculty, and are usually acted on by the academic officers to whom the library reports. They are reviewed annually and revised as necessary. Published and made available to students and faculty, they usually address such topics as: collection development, access, organization, preservation and storage, lending, audiovisual production, reference and instruction, facilities and equipment, cooperative activities, finances, staffing, management methods, and values.

Figure 3.3 is a worksheet that can be completed to define the input, outcome, and process goals the library is seeking to implement.

Objectives

Objectives are specific statements that define the library's tasks and timetables for meeting its goals. Two basic types of performance objectives are defined: maintenance objectives and project objectives.

Maintenance objectives define the tasks necessary to perform ongoing, routine functions. They are repeated regularly and determine major portions of annual plans and staff assignments.

Project objectives define tasks related to key issues and are targeted to develop, extend, or improve functions, policies, procedures, and programs. Projects are essential to growth, innovation, and change.

Both types of objectives:

1. Are explicit and expressed so that progress toward the achievement can be monitored or measured.
2. Include dimensions of time and performance expectations.
3. Reflect immediate, short-term, and long-range planning.

Objectives are drafted by the library staff and acted on by the library's management team. They are reviewed at least annually, but progress toward them is regularly monitored or measured and reported.

Figure 3.4 is a worksheet to help define the maintenance and project objectives necessary to achieve one of the defined goals.

Figure 3.5 is a sample of maintenance and project objectives developed to address one goal, in this case collection development. The objectives describe activities, timetables, persons responsible, and feedback mechanisms for decision making. Note the objectives define collection development assignments for the entire library staff including reference, circulation, interlibrary loan, cataloging, and administration, in addition to acquisitions staff.

The Accreditation Self-Study Report

A copy of the current library's mission and goals statement is usually included in the library section of an accreditation self-study report. The text also identifies how these statements are made available to the campus community. Depending upon the nature of the accreditation review and whether the library is a special emphasis, the entire statement of objectives may not be appropriate for inclusion in the report. However, it is readily available to accrediting team members, and instructions for obtaining a complete copy of the objectives are noted in the report.

Additional Readings

For more information about preparing a statement of mission, goals and objectives, consult the following sources:

Hastreiter, Jamie Webster, Larry Hardesty, and David Henderson, comps. *Mission Statements for College Libraries.* Clip Notes #5. Chicago: ACRL, 1985.

McClure, Charles R. and others. *Planning and Role Setting for Public Libraries: A Manual of Options and Procedures.* Chicago: American Library Association, 1987.

Popham, W. James. *Educational Evaluation.* Englewood Cliffs, N.J.: Prentice-Hall, 1975.

FIGURE 3.1   Mission Worksheet

The parent institution the library serves is: _____

The mission of the institution is: _____

The characteristics of the institution's community are:

_____ Students   _____ Instructional programs

_____ Faculty   _____ Research

_____ Other constituants

The purpose of the library is: _____

The philosophy of the library is: _____

The people who compose this statement are: _____

The people who review this statement are: _____

The people who approve this statement are: _____

The date this statement was adopted: _____

The date this statement will be reviewed: _____

FIGURE 3.2   Sample Accreditation Report Excerpt and
                     Mission Statement

In 1990 with the approval of the College Executive Committee, the Library adopted this statement of mission and goals:

The mission of Our College Library is to provide information resources and services that support the College's mission of teaching and scholarly inquiry to promote liberal learning, education for service, training for careers, and the development of life-long learning skills. We serve a culturally diverse student body of 1200 full-time and over 1000 part-time students, 70 percent of whom are over the age of twenty-five. While most students are academically talented, the college has committed itself to providing educational opportunities to 100 promising students with poor academic preparation. We aim to provide quality, cost-effective information services that are sufficiently flexible to meet the challenges of educational, societal, and technological change.

The goals of the library are:

1. To select materials and develop collections that are appropriate to the college's curricular programs and responsive to student and faculty needs and abilities;
2. To organize for use, store, and preserve information in any format that supports the college's teaching and research missions;
3. To provide access to information stored in libraries, repositories, and databases worldwide and distributed in print and electronically, and to teach the academic community how to find and select the information they need effectively and efficiently;
4. To support and promote the use of information resources by providing lending, instruction, and consultative services that meet the needs of individuals and classroom groups;
5. To produce audiovisual materials supporting the college's teaching programs;
6. To accommodate users, collections, and staff in facilities that are conducive to study, work, and preservation of materials, and available for use at appropriate hours.
7. To support and participate in local, regional, and national programs that make available on a collective basis library resources and services to those engaged in learning, teaching, and research.
8. To increase the level of funding available to the library by participating in fundraising and grant-seeking activities.
9. To employ, develop, and retain qualified and service-oriented staff capable individually and collectively of achieving these goals and program objectives.
10. To use appropriate management methods that ensure optimal use of human, physical, and financial resources; and the development, implementation, and evaluation of services and programs in the context of changing institutional, technological, and fiscal conditions.

FIGURE 3.2 (Continued)

In response to the 1989 revision of the Mission of the College the above statement was developed from a draft prepared by the library staff and reviewed by the Library Advisory Committee membership of two students, two faculty members, and one administrator. It is included in the library handbook which is distributed to all faculty and students. The library formally reviews this statement in consultation with the Library Advisory Committee every five years in accordance with the College's five-year cycle for reviewing the Mission of the College. The library staff uses this library mission and goals statement to develop an annual statement of objectives which specifies strategies and schedules for achieving the above goals. A copy of this complete statement of mission, goals, and objectives is available from the Library Director's Office.

FIGURE 3.3   Goals Worksheet

Input goals

Define the resources and services the library aims to provide (collections, preservation, storage, organization, lending, reference, instruction, audiovisual production, facilities, equipment, access to off-campus information services, staffing).

_____

_____

_____

_____

_____

Outcome goals

Define the achievements the library aims to promote (information usage, research skills, learning, research, community service, professional development of college faculty and staff, inter-institutional cooperation, finances and fund-raising).

_____

_____

_____

_____

_____

Process goals

Define the management methods and values the library aims to employ (cost-effective operations, management styles compatible with college requirements, currency with technological change, fiscal soundness).

_____

_____

_____

_____

_____

FIGURE 3.4   Objectives Worksheet

---

1. Define the goal:

   _____

   _____

   _____

2. Define maintenance objectives (those tasks that are necessary to perform the routine, ongoing functions associated with the goal). For each explicitly define:

   The task that must be accomplished: _____

   _____

   The person(s)/department responsible for the task: _____

   _____

   The time frame and/or standard of quality that must be met: _____

   _____

   The method and timetable that is used to monitor, report progress: _____

   _____

   _____

3. Define project objectives (those tasks related to key issues and are targeted to develop, extend, or improve functions, policies, procedures, and programs related to the goal; they are scheduled in recognition of the assignments and time required by maintenance objectives).

   For each objective explicitly define: _____

   _____

   The task that must be accomplished: _____

   _____

   The person(s)/department responsible for the task: _____

   _____

   The time frame and/or standard of quality that must be met: _____

   _____

   The method and timetable that is used to monitor and report progress:

   _____

   _____

FIGURE 3.5   Sample Goal and Objectives of Our Library

Goal: To select materials and develop collections that are appropriate to the college's curricular programs, and responsive to student and faculty needs and abilities.

Maintenance objectives

1. *To determine student and faculty needs:*

The reference staff annually collects syllabi of all courses and examines them for content, noting in particular assignments that should provoke library use. The collection development policy for that subject area is updated to reflect any changes.

The circulation and interlibrary loan staff annually examines circulation and interlibrary loan data to determine what materials are in demand by students and faculty. The collection development policy for those subject areas is updated to reflect any changes.

Every two years the library conducts a survey of its users; the biennial survey alternately samples faculty and students (i.e., each group is surveyed every fourth year). User need and satisfaction with the collection are among the areas investigated by this survey. The results are used to update collection development policies.

The reference staff interviews faculty involved with library instruction programs about their views of the collection and suggestions for improvement; this information is used to update collection development policies.

Suggestions for addition to the collection made by faculty and students via the suggestion box or staff contact are forwarded to the acquisitions staff for action.

On a rotating basis every eight years, all library department liaisons are asked to meet with a library staff member to review the appropriate subject statement in the collection development policies for possible revision in light of the department's course syllabi and research interests as documented by publications, grant applications, study leave applications, annual faculty research plans, etc. Standard bibliographies and recommended lists may be reviewed to support this effort. Three or four of the academic department policies are reviewed each year.

2. *To build a balanced collection of information in all formats and subject areas, library material budgets are targeted for allocation as follows: 40 percent books, 40 percent subscriptions, 10 percent audiovisuals and microforms, 10 percent computer software.*

Each year two-thirds of the book budget is allocated among subject areas using an index based on use, price, and number of titles reviewed in subject fields. The allocations are for the selection of current imprints. Additionally, three or four disciplines receive a doubled allocation to address collection development goals identified as part of the collection policy review cycle. One-third of the book budget supports selections by the library staff.

FIGURE 3.5 (Continued)

The acquisitions staff informs library departmental liaisons of the status of their allocation on a monthly basis throughout the academic year. All allocations must be fully encumbered by March 1; any remaining unencumbered balances revert to the library's general fund on March 1.

The acquisitions staff maintains records on price by subject area, and number of titles reviewed in subject areas to support the formula-driven allocation process.

The budgets for subscriptions, nonprints, and computer software are not allocated to subject areas. Suggestions for purchases are sought from academic departments; requests must describe course-related needs and are evaluated by the library staff in light of those needs and past use.

3. *To support faculty and library staff to remain current in the selection process:*

The acquisitions staff routes to appropriate faculty and staff publisher's announcements, blurbs, lists of outstanding new publications, etc.

The periodicals staff routes to appropriate faculty and staff selection tools such as *Choice, Library Journal*, etc.

Staff assigned selection responsibilities remain current and review all selection tools within one week of receipt.

Faculty and staff are guided in their selection activities by collection development policies developed cooperatively between the library and the departments. These policy statements are updated as necessary, at least once every eight years. They briefly describe the curricular and research demands in the subject area; existing strengths and weakness of the collection; and guidelines for collection intensity in the various subdivisions of the discipline.

4. *To remove worn, outdated, and unnecessary material from the collection:*

The library staff examines 10 percent of the collection each year to identify materials that might be candidates for weeding based on the following guidelines:

Material has been available for use for at least 10 years,
Material has never circulated and shows no signs of in-house use,
Material has been used less than three times in the last 10 years and not at all in the last 5 years,
Material meets the above criteria and also does not appear on the "standard lists."

Materials that meet all of the above criteria are included in a list of potential withdrawals and circulated to faculty for review. Those that have no redeeming value are withdrawn.

Materials that are identified as worn beyond use but of continuing value are reported to the acquisitions department for replacement and withdrawal upon receipt.

(Continued)

FIGURE 3.5   (Continued)

5. *To evaluate the quality of the collection and its effectiveness in meeting student and faculty needs:*

The cataloging staff annually reports the following data:

Total number of units by type of material,
Number of units added by type of material,
Number of units added/per capita,
Number of units added by subject of material.

The acquisitions staff annually reports the following data:

Expenditure by type of material,
Expenditure by subject of material,
Expenditure/per capita.

The circulation staff annually reports the following data:

Circulation data by status of borrower,
Circulation data by subject (a factor in the formula for allocating book budget),
Circulation data by type of material,
Circulation data per capita,
Circulation penetration data,
In-library pick-up data,
Collection turnover: rate number of circ/number of units held,
Number of registered borrowers by type of borrowers,
Percent of target populations who are borrowers,
Ratio of circulation/interlibrary loan transactions,
Every five years the library conducts an availability/accessibility study.

6. *To evaluate the effectiveness selection and acquisitions processes:*

The acquisitions staff aims to:

Process all requests for purchase within one week of receipt,
Process all incoming materials and make available to cataloging within 48 hours of receipt,
Process all invoices within 48 hours of receipt,
Acknowledge and process all gifts to the collection within one month of receipt depending upon size of the donation.

The acquisitions staff annually collects the following data:

Percent of eligible faculty recommending purchases,
Number and amount of funds unencumbered by March 1 deadline,
Number and percent of faculty requests that represent items already owned,
Number and percent of faculty requests that are not owned and are met,

FIGURE 3.5   (Concluded)

Average cost of acquiring various types of material from receipt of request
to completed handling by acquisitions,
Average elapsed time between receipt of request for purchase to receipt of
material and availability for use,
Vendor performance data.

Project objectives for the coming year
(Including periodic maintenance objectives scheduled this year.)

1. Quadrennial faculty user survey to be conducted in spring semester.
2. Political science, military science, and history collection policy reviews are
   scheduled this year.
3. LC classification H is scheduled for inventory and weeding summer semester.
4. Library staff will work with the staff of the Academic Assistance Center
   which is established to address the retention goals enumerated in the
   college strategic plan. We will define a collection development policy
   statement to support the information needs of students identified as de-
   ficient in study and basic skills. This policy statement will be completed
   by April 1 so that budget allocation can reflect the collection development
   plan to serve these students.
5. The library's rare book collection is targeted in the college strategic plan as
   a priority for development to help us maintain our ranking in our institutional peer group. In the coming year, the acquisitions staff and the
   director's office will devote particular attention to strengthening the Heritage Collection. A major collection has been targeted for potential be-
   quest, and funds to support and maintain the entire Heritage Collection
   will be solicited.

SECTION II: Performance Evaluation

The driving force behind the library's management, self-study, and accreditation processes is the evaluation of its performance in carrying out its mission. The library implements ongoing assessment processes to monitor, analyze, and document the extent to which it is achieving its goals and objectives. The key ingredients in effective performance evaluation are: routinely collected data; special studies; and summative interpretive reports that assess progress, inform decisions and bring about desired improvements, and impact future goals and objectives.

Routinely Collected Data

For each goal and objective the library pursues, the library defines the data that it routinely assembles on an ongoing basis to document progress. Collecting meaningful and reliable data is a key activity in the library's assessment process, and the data should be consistent and stable. The goals and objectives that are most readily monitored by ongoing recorded data collection are input goals and objectives, those that define the resources and services the library provides. In particular, routine data collection is employed to monitor goals that relate to collection development; organization, preservation, and storage; audiovisual production; facilities and equipment; cooperative activities; and finances and staffing. Ongoing data collection also monitors selected output goals and objectives that define services the library promotes, for example, usage data related to lending, reference, and instruction.

Special Studies

Special studies are used to evaluate progress toward goals and objectives when:

1. Ongoing data collection is prohibited by costs associated with its collection such as staff time, equipment, or resources.
2. Ongoing data collection is prohibited because it intrudes on patron service, time, convenience, or comfort.
3. Progress cannot be measured by ongoing data collection, but it can be evaluated by methods such as interviews, attitude surveys, etc.
4. Routine data collection is of such a cumbersome nature that sampling is preferred for validity and reliability.
5. They can be conducted in compliance with regulations concerning the conduct of research involving human subjects.

The goals and objectives that are readily monitored by special studies are those outcome or process goals and objectives that relate to user impact or costs of collection development, instruction, and reference; management methods and values; patron needs, attitudes, or opinions. The set of output measures described in ACRL's *Measuring Academic Library Performance: A Practical Approach* are examples of the special kinds of studies that can be undertaken. The reading list at the end of this chapter suggests works on special studies involving collection development and public services that might be implemented as well.

Summative Interpretive Reports

The library periodically needs to analyze the results of its ongoing data collection efforts and special studies to make summative assessments of progress toward its goals and objectives. Such reports can take the form of annual reports in which major achievements and issues are highlighted. They might also be working papers in which progress toward one or more particular goals or long-term trends are assessed. The library section of the accreditation report, done on a ten-year cycle, is an example of a trend-line report.

The key ingredients of all such reports are:

1. A combination of routinely collected data and special reports.
2. A documented relationship between goals, objectives, and performance.
3. Historical trends that provide perspective.
4. Analysis of the comparative position with recognized standards, national norms, or position among cohort institutions.
5. Identification of impact of performance results on future plans; requirements for corrective action; expectations for, or obstacles to, continued performance.

As with routine, ongoing data collection and special studies, the library determines which summative reports will be produced by identifying:

1. Decisions that will be impacted by the information.
2. Reporting requirements to outside agencies.
3. Standards established by outside agencies.
4. Comparative reports available from cohort institutions.
5. Costs of information collection or preparation and available resources to meet them.

Figure 3.6 is a worksheet that will help the library to determine what data, special studies, or interpretative reports should be undertaken. It assists the library in defining the purpose and costs associated with the assessment activities being considered.

Once requirements for data collection, special studies, or summative reports are identified, the library defines:

1. Procedures used to collect, analyze, and report information.
2. Staff responsible for collection, analysis, and reporting.
3. Persons who are to receive resulting reports.
4. Timetables for collection, analysis, and reporting.
5. Schedule for reviewing the need to continue such activities.

The above information is recorded in staff policy and procedures manuals for continuing reference.

The Accreditation Self-Study Report

The library section of the institution's accreditation self-study report is an example of a summative interpretative report. Its description of the library's performance usually includes the following information:

1. A summary of the major accomplishments achieved in addressing its goal during the past three to five years.
2. A summary of the major obstacles or indicators of concern that have impeded progress toward major objectives, with recommendations as to how they might be addressed.
3. Evidence of strategic planning, the development of library service over a three- to five-year range.
4. A brief description of the processes used to assess progress toward the library's goals and objectives, including a schedule of special studies.
5. Instructions for obtaining more detailed explanations and results of various assessment techniques being employed by the library. This could be references to appendices with more detailed statistical reports, or supplementary reports and documents available for consultation by interested parties.

While specific institutional goals and objectives dictate methods of assessment and reporting of results, tradition and national standards would suggest accreditation reports should include as appendices or have available in background documents the following routinely collected performance data: (1) collection development and usage, (2) reference and instruction contacts, (3) facilities and equipment usage, (4) cooperative activities, (5) finances, and (6) staffing. See sample data tables in figures 3.7, 3.8, and 3.9 for further details.

Special studies and summative, interpretative reports related to:

1. Student and faculty information needs: circulation data, inventory loss data, in-library usage data, external document delivery data, syllabi studies, faculty interviews, interlibrary loan usage studies, user requests, and surveys of faculty and students including part-time.
2. Student and faculty assessment of library performance: student and faculty surveys and focus group interviews.
3. Collection quality and its impact on student and faculty performance: comparisons with standard or recommended lists of materials; user surveys; analysis of interlibrary loan requests; ratios of interlibrary loans to circulation; and citation availability studies using student and faculty papers and publications as a base.
4. The library instructional program quality and its impact on student or faculty performance: faculty and student surveys; student performance on library assignments and tests; examination of student papers to determine effect of instruction on results; change in foregoing results as students progress from freshman thru senior years; and repeat requests for instruction.
5. Time and cost studies of key library functions: average cost and time to get book on shelf from time of request to time of availability to user; average cost and time to complete interlibrary loan from time of request to time item is available to user; average cost and time of circulation transaction; average cost and time expended on reference transaction and online searches; average cost and time expended on bibliographic instruction/capita exposed; and staff turnover.

The above data offer a microlevel analysis of library effectiveness of primary value for internal formative evaluation aimed at analyzing and improving library services and operations. Lost in such detail is the macrolevel summative assessment that is valuable for both internal and external judgments of overall effectiveness. This summative assessment is conveyed by highlighting a very few measures in the main body of the accreditation report. These few measures are:

1. Circulation by patron category.
2. Per capita circulation by patron category.
3. Circulation penetration by patron category, i.e., the number of actual different borrowers in each category divided by the total number of persons (potential borrowers) in the patron category.

4. Interlibrary loan transactions by patron category.
5. Per capita interlibrary loan transaction by patron category.
6. Interlibrary loan transaction penetration by patron category, i.e., the number of different users in each category divided by the total number of persons (potential users) in the patron category.
7. Electronic document delivery transactions by patron category.
8. Per capita electronic document delivery transactions by patron category.
9. Electronic document delivery penetration by patron category, i.e., the number of different users in each category divided by the total number of persons (potential users) in patron category.
10. Reference transaction by patron category.
11. Per capita reference transaction by patron category.
12. Reference transaction penetration by patron category, i.e., the number of different users in each category by the total number of persons (potential users) in the patron category.
13. Instructional contacts by patron category.
14. Per capita instructional contact by patron category.
15. Instructional contact penetration by patron category, i.e., the number of different persons in each category receiving library instruction divided by the total number of persons (potential users) in the patron category.

The above fifteen categories of data presented in the context of historical trends and comparative cohort data are summary indicators of library performance. Most other data is of diagnostic value in explaining these summative indicators.

The "penetration" data described above have not routinely been reported by libraries. The term "penetration" is used in the sense of "market penetration." That is, of the potential market for a given service, what percentage of that market is being reached? In the context of higher education data, penetration data have counterparts in other units of the institution that make them understandable to an administrative audience, e.g., yield data from the admissions office; retention data from the dean's office; and percentage of alumni donors from the development office.

Additional Readings

Baker, Sharon L. and Frederick W. Lancaster. *The Measurement and Evaluation of Library Services*. 2nd ed. Arlington, Virginia: Information Resources Press, 1991.

Cronin, Mary J. *Performance Measurement for Public Services in Academic and Research Libraries.* Washington, D.C.: Association of Research Libraries, 1985.

Ferguson, Anthony W. and others. "The RLG Conspectus: Its Uses and Benefits." *College and Research Libraries* 49 (May 1988): 197–206.

Hafner, Arthur W. *Descriptive Statistical Techniques for Librarians.* Chicago and London: American Library Association, 1989.

Hall, Blaine H. *Collection Assessment Manual for College and University Libraries.* Phoenix, Arizona: Oryx Press, 1985.

Jakubs, Deborah. *Qualitative Collection Analysis: The Conspectus Methodology.* SPEC Kit 151. Washington, D.C.: Association of Research Libraries, 1980.

Kania, Antoinette M. "Academic Library Standards and Performance Measures." *College and Research Libraries* 49 (January 1988): 16–23.

Kania, Antoinette M. *Performance Measures for Academic Libraries: A Twenty Year Retrospective.* Eric Document No. ED 293540, 8 pp. Bethesda, Maryland: ERIC, 1988.

McClure, Charles R. and others. *A New Strategic Direction for the AAHSLD Annual Statistics: Planning, Service Roles, Performance Measures and Management Information Systems for Academic Health Sciences Libraries: Final Report for Phase I.* Houston: Association of Academic Health Sciences Library Directors, 1991.

Shapiro, Beth J. "Access and Performance Measures in Research Libraries." *Journal of Library Administration* 15 (1991): 49–66.

Swisher, Robert and Charles R. McClure. *Research for Decision Making: Methods for Librarians.* Chicago and London: American Library Association, 1984.

Van House, Nancy, Beth T. Weil, and Charles R. McClure. *Measuring Academic Library Performance: A Practical Approach.* Chicago and London: American Library Association, 1990.

Sources for Statistical Information

Library statistics provide information identifying trends and rankings that will help place the library in perspective. Descriptive statistical studies identifying the library's standing within a peer group are useful goal-setting tools. The institution's academic officers should be consulted in the selection of a peer group. Institutional memberships in data collection and analysis services may be available to assist the library to compile comparative reports.

The following listings identify major sources of published data and data collection and analysis services. In addition, librarians should check the publications of state library associations and network agencies as a number of them conduct surveys and report the results. The Pennsylvania Library Association's annual *Salary Survey of Pennsylvania Academic Libraries* is an example, following the ARL salary survey model. Data publications are rapidly outdated, and the most current authoritative sources should be employed in interpreting the library's performance.

Publications

ACRL/Historically Black Colleges and Universities Library Statistics, 1988–89. Chicago: ACRL, 1991.

ACRL University Library Statistics, 1990–91. Chicago: ACRL, 1992.

ARL Annual Salary Survey, 1991. Washington, D.C.: Association of Research Libraries, 1992.

ARL Statistics 1990–91. Washington, D.C.: Association of Research Libraries, 1992.

Academic and Public Librarians: Data by Race, Ethnicity and Sex. Chicago and London: American Library Association, 1991.

Academic Library Survey: 1990 Institution Response. Boulder, Colorado: John Minter Associates, 1993.

Bowker Annual of Library and Book Trade Information, 1993. Chicago and New York: R. R. Bowker, 1993.

Creal, Richard C. and others. *1992–93 Administrative Compensation Survey.* Washington, D. C.: College and University Personnel Association, 1993.

Lynch, Mary Jo and others. *ALA Survey of Librarian Salaries, 1992.* Chicago and London: American Library Association, 1993.

Molyneux, Robert E. (compiler). *Academic Library Statistics, 1978/79–1988/89 (Diskettes).* Chicago: ACRL, 1989.

Statistical Norms for College and University Libraries Fall 1988. 2nd ed. Boulder, Colorado: John Minter Associates, 1990.

Data Collection and Analysis Services

A number of individuals and organizations have developed statistical collection and analysis instruments and the references have grown steadily in recent years. The suggestions below are not intended to be all-inclusive but simply to illustrate the variety of available materials. Librarians may find Patrick Dewey's *202 (+) Software Packages to Use in Your Library: Descriptions, Evaluations and Practical Advice* a useful guide in identifying software to support the analysis and reporting project.

The specialized programmatic accrediting bodies are developing their own guidelines and instruments for accreditation reviews. Libraries at institutions holding one or more forms of specialized accreditation should be certain to have current publications from each accrediting body with which it is affiliated that are relevant to data-driven evaluations and assessments.

Associated Colleges of the Midwest
  c/o Sarah M. McGowan
  Ripon College Library
  300 Seward Street
  P.O. Box 248
  Ripon, WI 54971-1499

National Data Service for Higher Education
  John Minter Associates
  2400 Central Avenue B-2
  Boulder, CO 80301

Oberlin Group Library Data
  72 Selective Colleges
  c/o Larry J. Frye
  Lilly Library
  Wabash College
  Crawfordsville, IN 47933

Systems and Procedures Exchange Center (SPEC)
  Association of Research Libraries
  Office of Management Studies
  1527 New Hampshire Avenue, N.W.
  Washington, DC 20036

Tufts-EDUCOM Project
  Higher Education Data Sharing Consortium
  c/o James F. Trainer
  Franklin & Marshall College
  Old Main 201
  P.O. Box 3003
  Lancaster, PA 17604-3003

FIGURE 3.6   Data, Special Study, Interpretive Report Worksheet

For each data collection activity, special study, or interpretative report, complete the following worksheet to determine if it is to be implemented or continued. In conducting this exercise, keep these questions in mind: Why is the data collected? How is it used? Does its use help the library improve its services? Would other data be more helpful?

Describe activity, study, or report:

1. Identify the performance goal, objective, or activity this information assesses. _____

_____

_____

2. Identify the decision the information impacts. _____

_____

_____

3. Identify the external agency that requires the information._____

_____

_____

4. Identify the external agency standard it addresses. _____

_____

_____

5. Identify comparative data available from cohort institutions. _____

_____

6. Identify the cost of the activity and available resources to cover cost. ___

_____

7. Identify the impact on patron service, convenience, comfort, staff productivity, and morale. _____

_____

8. Determine if the activity is in compliance with regulations regarding research on human subjects. _____

_____

9. Decide if the information is necessary and/or worth it all. _____

_____

FIGURE 3.7 Performance Data Worksheets: Collection Development

	Performance Data: Collection Development Years						
	1	2	3	4	Current Year	Cohort Mean	Our Rank
INPUT MEASURES:							
Number of volumes							
Number of volumes added per year							
Number of volumes withdrawn/yr.							
Number of volumes/fte students							
Number of volumes added/year/fte students							
Number of active periodical subscriptions							
Number of microfilm reels							
Number of microfiche							
Number of microcards							
Number of non-print items:							
Audiodiscs							
Audiotapes							
Slides							

(Continued)

FIGURE 3.7 (Continued)

Performance Data: Collection Development

	Years				Current Year	Cohort Mean	Our Rank
	1	2	3	4			
Films							
Filmstrips							
Videotapes							
Computer Software							
Government publications							
Paper documents							
Microform documents							
Computer software							
Total materials, expenditures							
Total materials, expenditure/fte student							
Percent of library budget expended on materials							
Percent of materials budget expended on							
books							
periodicals							

FIGURE 3.7 (Continued)

Performance Data: Collection Development

	Years				Current Year	Cohort Mean	Our Rank
	1	2	3	4			
audiovisual							
computer software							
other (define)							
OUTPUT OR IMPACT MEASURES:							
Number of circulations							
Number of circulation/fte student							
Number of in-library uses							
Number of in-library uses/fte student							
Number of book circulations							
Number of microformat uses							
Number of periodical uses							
Number of software uses							
Ratio of circulation/number of ILL transactions							
Ratio of circulation/volumes held							

(Continued)

FIGURE 3.7 (Concluded)

Performance Data: Collection Development

	Years				Current Year	Cohort Mean	Our Rank
	1	2	3	4			
Penetration: Percentage of actual borrowers/total population:							
Faculty							
Students							
PROCESS MEASURES:							
Percent of faculty recommending purchases							
Number of faculty recommendations							
Percent of recommendations filled							
Average cost of acquiring and preparing materials for use							
Average time elapsed between recommendation for purchase and availability for use							

FIGURE 3.8 Performance Data Worksheets: Library Services

Performance Data: Library Services

	Years					Current Year	Cohort Mean	Our Rank
	1	2	3	4				
INPUT MEASURES:								
Hours of Service:								
Access to collections								
Reference services								
Lending services								
Interlibrary services								
Microcomputer services								
Online services								
Audiovisual services								
Promotional activities:								
Bibliographies								
Displays								
Facilities								
Number of user spaces								
Percent of students seated								
Number of microcomputers								

(Continued)

FIGURE 3.8 (Continued)

Performance Data: Library Services

	Years				Current Year	Cohort Mean	Our Rank
	1	2	3	4			
Number of microform readers							
Number of microprinters							
Number of photocopiers							
Number of film projectors							
Number of VCRs							
Linear feet of shelving							
Percent of shelving occupied							
Number of catalog access terminals							
OUTPUT OR IMPACT MEASURES:							
Number of user questions received							
Number of user questions answered							
Number of questions/fte students							
Number of online searches							
Number of online searches/fte students							
Number of library instruction classes							

FIGURE 3.8 (Continued)

Performance Data: Library Services

	Years				Current Year	Cohort Mean	Our Rank
	1	2	3	4			
Percentage of students reached by library instruction program							
Number of registered borrowers							
Students							
/percent of total							
Faculty							
/percent of total							
Other							
Number of interlibrary loan transactions							
Number of items borrowed							
Number of items loaned							
Penetration of ILL: Number of borrowers/percent of total in each target population, percent of faculty users, percent of student users.							
Number of photocopier uses							

(Continued)

FIGURE 3.8 (Concluded)

Performance Data: Library Services

	Years				Current Year	Cohort Mean	Our Rank
	1	2	3	4			
Number of microcomputer uses							
Number of audiovisual equipment uses							
PROCESS MEASURES:							
Average cost of interlibrary loan transactions							
Average turnaround time for interlibrary loan transactions							
Fulfillment percentage for interlibrary loans							
Average cost of circulation transactions							
Average cost of online transactions							
Average cost of reference transactions							

FIGURE 3.9 Performance Data Worksheets: Administrative Services

Performance Data: Administrative Services

	Years				Current Year	Cohort Mean	Our Rank
	1	2	3	4			
INPUT MEASURES:							
Number of library staff							
Professional staff							
Technical staff							
Clerical staff							
Student staff							
Librarian/fte student							
Total salaries							
Total wages							
Total equipment							
Total supplies							
Total income from grants							
Total income from gifts							

SECTION III: Organizational Skills

Once the library has in place an ongoing system of defining its goals and objectives, and regular data collection and analysis routines for assessing its performance, it can deal with the accreditation process as an opportunity, not a threat. However, even in the best managed environment, the accreditation process can encounter pitfalls if some basic organizational skills are not honed and applied. The most common of these organizational issues are dealt with in this final section on communication and meetings.

Communication

Communication problems are caused by a variety of circumstances and occurrences within an accrediting review. The most common causes include differing perceptions as to the goals and objectives of the accrediting review. Even when objectives are clearly articulated they may be perceived differently by various participants. Secondly, there may be different expectations regarding actions to be taken on results of the review. Competition for funds, facilities, and personnel are threats to open communciations and will lead to conflicts. Finally, personal antagonisms or personality conflicts strain communications links. Some of these pre-existing conditions are carried into the review process. Others are generated by persons who perceive the tasks of the study team as threats to their authority or status.

Maintaining effective communication links in an accrediting study can be difficult and troublesome. It involves considerable time and interpersonal skills on the part of the study team and units such as the library. Many study team chairs find that they spend half of their time talking to study participants, getting information, clarifying directions, and resolving conflicts and misunderstandings. Much of the time is involved with the responsibility for maintaining communications links both within and outside the study in order to assure integration of the study and a cohesive report.

The personal factor in handling communications problems is usually more crucial than the structural, organizational, or methodological ones. The choice of study team leader is crucial for the institution, as is the choice of the accreditation project officer for the library. They can help ensure that the following key ingredients to minimizing communications difficulties are in place: good planning; clearly written charges; tasks lists and timetables; careful recording of decisions; and training in self-study processes and group dynamics. They can also ensure that all appropriate reports are widely circulated, and confidentiality is appropriately maintained. Such actions build trust that makes for effective communication.

Ineffective Meetings

"All we do is go to meetings and nothing ever happens; this whole accreditation thing is a waste of time and money." When the accreditation process goes "bad," this is the most frequent expression of institutional frustration and failure. Frequently, the complaint about meetings is a symptom of deeper problems with planning, communication, or resistance to change. Often it is a legitimate complaint about ineffective, time-wasting meetings. There is a vast literature about making meetings work that can be briefly summarized in the following cardinal rules:

1. Always have an agenda and distribute it to participants in advance of the meeting. An agenda determines what is to be accomplished and who is needed to accomplish it. Make sure it lists times, date, place, duration, participants, objectives of the meetings, and topics to be addressed. Be as brief as possible, preferably one page. Append essential background information. For a sample agenda format see figure 3.10.
2. Include only those people who need to be there. The nature of the meeting identifies who they are—usually the people who work closely with some aspect of the agenda's key topics.
3. Meet for no more than two hours.
4. Start the meeting and end the meeting on time.
5. Be upbeat in getting the meeting started; do not apologize for yet another meeting. There is important business to be done, and everyone involved is needed to get it done. It has been planned that way.
6. Summarize the results of the meetings and distribute them to all participants. Make sure the summary includes a clearly defined task list with assignments, responsible parties, and due dates. See figure 3.11 for a sample meeting summary format.
7. Train chairs or leaders in group dynamics: successful seating arrangements, stimulating and balancing discusssions, dealing with hidden agendas, encouraging or limiting participation and reaching consensus and closure.

Whether or not the library and its parent institution espouse total quality management (TQM) philosophy and style, the processes of TQM are helpful in producing more effective meetings. In particular, the TQM literature offers excellent guidance on forming and training teams and their leaders. Accreditation data collection and program analysis could be aided by TQM's basic tools for problem identification and analysis, for example flow charts, force field analysis, pareto charts, affinity diagrams, and prioritization matrices. Much of the TQM literature provides good advice on conducting meetings, developing listening skills, resolving conflicts, and applying common sense to group efforts. The reading list includes examples of these publications.

Additional Readings

Bradford, Leland P. *Making Meetings Work: A Guide for Leaders and Group Members.* LaJolla, Calif.: University Associates, 1976.

Brassard, Michael. *The Memory Jogger™.* Methuen, Mass.: Goal/QPC, 1988.

————. *The Memory Jogger + ™.* Metheun, Mass.: Goal/QPC, 1989.

Katz, Daniel and Robert Kahn. *Social Psychology of Organizations.* 2nd ed. New York: Wiley, 1978.

Kieffer, George David. *The Strategy of Meetings.* New York: Simon and Schuster, 1988.

The Memory Jogger™ For Educators. Methuen, Mass.: Goal/QPC, 1992.

Scholtes, Peter R. and others. *The Team Handbook.* Madison, Wisconsin: Joiner Associates, Inc., 1988.

FIGURE 3.10   Sample Agenda Format

Date: _____

_____

_____

Time: (start and ending) _____

_____

_____

Place: _____

_____

_____

Participants: _____

_____

_____

Objectives: _____

_____

_____

_____

Topics: _____

_____

_____

_____

Preparation required: _____

_____

_____

_____

List of background attachments: _____

_____

_____

_____

_____

FIGURE 3.11   Sample Meeting Summary Form

Date: _____

Time: _____

Participants: _____

_____

_____

_____

_____

Topics addressed: _____

_____

_____

_____

_____

Decisions reached: _____

_____

_____

_____

_____

Assignments: _____

_____

_____

_____

_____

Tasks	Responsible party	Due date
_____	_____	_____
_____	_____	_____
_____	_____	_____
_____	_____	_____

Chapter Four   Using Accreditation Results

While the planning, preparation, and ongoing management processes outlined in the previous chapters are the key ingredients in the accreditation process, the on-site visit of the agency's evaluation team and the institution's response to the agency's report are the transforming events in any review. Once the self-study has been conducted, effective utilization of its findings must begin with a successful interaction with the evaluation team during the team visit. The accreditation visit and the institution's responses to it are briefly reviewed in the first part of this chapter. However, our primary focus is on the library's participation in the visit and the utilization of accreditation results to satisfy the library's agenda for improvement.

The Accreditation Visit and Responses at the Institutional Level

The stages of institution's responses to the accrediting agency's visit usually include:

1. Receiving and responding to the agency's suggested evaluation team roster.
2. Distributing the institution's report or self-study, the catalog, faculty and student handbooks, and related materials to the evaluation team members and the accrediting agency.
3. Preparing for the team visit. These preparations usually include: travel arrangements and housing for the team; defining a schedule that includes getting acquainted events and oral reports, interviews with trustees, college officers, faculty, students and staff; and on-campus support that includes access to background document files and secretarial assistance.

4. Hosting the team's visit. Discussing the review or self-study, sharing experiences, and responding to questions and perceptions of the evaluation team.
5. Receiving an oral preview of the team's evaluation report.
6. Responding officially to the team's report. This written brief, together with the self-study and the team's report, is considered by the accrediting agency in determining its action.
7. Responding to the agency's formal accrediting action. Some actions may require no follow-up activities except for routine periodic reports, e.g., reaffirmation of accreditation without conditions. Other actions may request follow-up reports or another on-site evaluation. In each case requiring a follow-up activity, the accrediting agency defines the focus of these requirements, the institution's responsibilities and timetable for response.

Of more than equal importance are the institution's commitment and activities that act on the results of its accrediting review or self-study, and the advice it receives from the accrediting team's report, and the agency's action. Considerable time and attention are given to most evaluation reviews, and the results of such efforts should be seriously considered in the planning and decision-making processes. How to use the results of the accrediting review at an institutional level, particularly the relationship of self-study to planning has received considerable attention in the literature and will not be reviewed here. Instead the library's opportunities for use of these results are the focus of the next part of this chapter.

The Accreditation Visit and Responses at the Library Level

The library should seize the accreditation visit as an opportunity for consultancy, affirmation of direction, and new perspectives. The central question the evaluator seeks to answer is, "Does it work?" That is, does a given library program function effectively in light of the library's and the institution's stated goals? The atmosphere should not be one of inspection, examination, accountability, and fault finding. To avoid such an atmosphere in responding to the accreditation visit, the library utilizes the following strategy:

1. Anticipate that the review will be based on the library section in the review or self-study document; in particular on the key

recommendations and implementation plans and processes contained in the conclusion of the library's self-study report.

2. Focus on the library's stated objectives and its effectiveness in meeting them in its dialogue with the accrediting team.
3. Maintain complete open communication with the accrediting team members.
4. Expect the accrediting team to understand the library's mission, goals, and related activities as articulated in the self-study document.

In addition, the library is advised to engage in the following activities in response to the visit:

1. Recommend a librarian be one of the members of the visiting accrediting team. In making this recommendation, the library should be knowledgeable about the accrediting agency's policies and practices regarding team membership, and be in touch with the officers of its parent institution about their requisites for team membership. If a librarian is not on the visiting team, identify the team member who will be primarily responsible for reviewing the library.
2. Select and make available related library documents for background files accessible to the evaluation team. Identify and prepare to distribute any key document that may be in demand by team members. When the library is a focus of the accrediting report, or if the library is "atypical" in comparison to its peers, and the institution's report to the accrediting agency cannot include the library's full report and/or background documents, ask the institution's steering committee to mail the full report and background documents to the appropriate team member at least one month before the team visit.
3. Seek an opportunity to meet with the accrediting team members and campus colleagues in a social setting.
4. Share information about the evaluation visit and schedules with the library staff to prepare them to greet the visitors and offer them assistance.
5. Be readily available for meetings with team members and arrange individual or group staff meetings in response to team requests.
6. Attend the oral preview of the team's evaluation report, and discuss the preview with library staff and academic officers.
7. Review the accrediting agency's evaluation report and advise on library-related contents.

8. Assist the institution in responding to the agency's formal accrediting action requiring follow-up reports or special visits with a library emphasis.

To increase the usefulness of the accrediting reviews, the library should consider:

1. Addressing key concerns expressed by the library's users as a first priority.
2. Initiating implementation of key recommendations identified in the self-study report prior to accrediting visits and reports.
3. Identifying matters that will require the understanding and support of the institution's decision makers and communicating with this audience. The plan for involving these persons should identify who the decision makers will be, what information they will need, and when the information will be needed. Evaluations are more likely to be used if they relate to decision makers' concerns, are communicated clearly and concisely with an assessment of their impact, and are presented both verbally and in written form.
4. Linking the accrediting agency's evaluations with the library's and the institution's planning and resource allocation processes. It is important for the results to be linked to these decision-making processes, but unreasonable to expect the recommendations to be implemented in their "pure form." The results should be reviewed with multiple perspectives.
5. Communicating the library's response to the library's audiences. Accrediting reviews occur in a social and political environment in which various groups have vested interests in the evaluation process. If the results are to be used by these groups, communication among them is essential.
6. Maintaining flexibility to accommodate change in the accreditation process. It is impossible to design an accrediting review process that anticipates all the issues that need to be addressed and all the constituencies that need to be consulted. Recommendations and their priority ordering will need to be adjusted in the implementation process to adapt to changing environments and to cultivate expectations at a reasonable level.

Figure 4.1 offers a worksheet for developing a plan to address specific accrediting agency recommendations. It identifies the persons responsible for implementing the recommendations, defines the specific maintenance and project objectives, and lists resources required to address the recommendation. The plans and timetables for assessing progress toward implementation are clearly outlined.

When the review results are used, basic concerns about the consequences of their application will surface. In fact, these concerns often appear in the design stage of the evaluation review and effect, sometimes negatively, the design itself. Assumptions about decreasing budget support, eliminating a subject collection responsibility or service, and changing personnel are viewed as negative and threatening. They create distrusts and resentment. These situations should be recognized as common conditions in organizations undergoing change.

Change

When accreditation reviews are positive or supportive of the library's needs, their implementation comes easily and the results are usually beneficial. However, not all evaluations are positive for the library and its staff. For some, the report may contain new and "startling" information or findings that are denied. For others, "bad news" is discouraging or disorganizing.

The results may threaten perceptions of status and competence, service quality, or prestige and position. Staff members may combat these threats by denying, deferring, denigrating, or destroying the evaluation results. New stresses appear with recommendations for change, and resistance to change is to be expected. Recognize, however, that the well-managed library has established an environment that is conducive to the effective use of accreditation results. These conditions stated below will lend themselves to successful implementation of changes.

1. The library has performance goals in place. Therefore, it has a reference point by which to assess the accrediting agency's response and to determine if the agency's recommendations are appropriate or suited to its needs.
2. The library has identified priorities among its various goals and objectives and has a focus for addressing them. Everything the library needs and wants to do cannot be done at once and well. Problems arise when the library has not clarified the relative emphasis of what it does. Implementation of agency recommendations must take into account these priorities and emphases.
3. The library has an ongoing evaluation process in place that reduces anxiety levels and is not problem or crisis centered. This process reduces the number of surprises likely to come out of the agency report.

4. The library employs a variety of performance measures and quality indicators as a basis for assessing its strengths and limitations. Recommendations for change can be dealt with in light of these data, and do not depend solely on frequently competing socio-political pressures within the academic community.

In addition to these general environmental factors supportive of change, the following specific actions will help the library support a change process that is stimulated or mandated by the accrediting review.

1. Recognize and accept the fact that change usually incites some resistance.
2. Assess the ability of the proposed change to provide a benefit or improvement, "to work." Resistance to outcomes may be for good reason and it is crucial that outcomes be beneficial. The changes need to produce results and a successful experience for the users and staff. If the assessment is "it won't work," the library should report its conclusion to the appropriate institutional officer and identify a course of action and any requirements for reporting to the accrediting agency.
3. Identify the magnitude of change. Small-scale changes are easier to make than full-scale implementations.
4. Unless the library is a seasoned change maker, introduce changes on a small scale initially, involving the most supportive staff at the outset. Implement a change process incrementally and maintain flexibility in the implementation process.
5. Develop the staff's understanding of the need for the change. Provide accurate information that describes the need. Use communication mechanisms that are effective in sharing information and providing feedback.
6. Cultivate peer group motivation for the change. Momentum and critical mass are essential ingredients in effecting change, and peer group support will build coalitions to implement the change.
7. Identify and address the needs of individual library staff. Frequently, rewards must change to support new practices. This can mean recognition; revision and implementation of performance appraisal criteria and reinforcing messages, both explicit and symbolic, from the library's and the institution's leaders; and financial rewards. The single most important incentive to change is to reward those staff members who make effective change happen.

In summary the library will be most successful in addressing the accrediting agency's recommendations by maintaining good communications that encourage cooperation from the staff and user constituencies. Before making any change, it will explore the problem in depth, identifying the causes and collecting information to make sure it has the appropriate solutions. Before making any change, it will take the time to identify both the positive and negative effects (what if it doesn't work?). And when it does "make the change" it will monitor its action—put in place an appropriate data collection effort to catch errors, make adjustments, and determine if the change is successful.

Additional Readings

Curzon, Susan C. *Managing Change: A How-to-Do-It Manual for Planning, Implementing, and Evaluating Change in Libraries.* New York: Neal-Schuman Publishers, Inc., 1989.

Hughes, K. Scott and Daryl Conner. (eds.) *Managing Change in Higher Education: Preparing for the 21st Century.* Washington, D.C.: College and University Personnel Association, 1989.

Kanter, Rosabeth Moss, Barry A. Stein and Todd D. Jick. *The Challenge of Organizational Change: How Companies Experience It and Leaders Guide It.* New York: Macmillan, 1992.

Kells, H. R. *Self-Study Processes.* 3rd ed. New York: American Council on Education and Macmillan, 1988.

Lindquist, Jack. *Strategies for Changes.* Berkeley, Calif.: Pacific Soundings Press, 1978.

Patton, Michael Quinn. *Creative Evaluation.* Beverly Hills, Calif.: Sage Publications, 1981.

FIGURE 4.1   Plan for Implementing Agency Recommendations

An appointed group of library staff members reviews the agency recommendations and identifies priorities among them, consulting with other staff, administrators, faculty, and students as appropriate. The group identifies the resources necessary to address the recommendations, and the Library Director in consultation with the Academic Officer and appropriate faculty/student representatives selects those recommendations that will be implemented and assigns resources. The group outlines and monitors the plan for implementing each recommendation as follows:

Plan for Implementing Agency Recommendation

Recommendation: _____

_____

_____

Persons responsible for implementation: _____

_____

_____

Maintenance and/or project objectives defined for implementation: _____

_____

_____

Resources committed (identify type, amount, and administrative approval):

_____

_____

_____

Plans for assessment of progress on implementation (define monitoring methods, timetables, responsible parties): _____

_____

_____

_____

Reporting requirements (define content, frequency, audience): _____

_____

_____

_____

_____

Conclusion

The concept and practices of accreditation are not without their challengers. Persons with varying political agendas are dissatisfied with the perceived politics of accreditation criteria and processes. A public distrustful of higher education in general doubts the integrity of the academy and its capacity to "police" itself. Even supporters of the accreditation concept fear the costs of implementing it are becoming too burdensome to bear. Many institutions seem to simultaneously downplay its importance and defend its vital role. While discussions about radically altering the process seem continuous, accreditation persists because no satisfactory alternative process has garnered consensus support. Until a viable alternative has been endorsed, accreditation will continue to be a major event in the life of an academic institution. Even if, or when, an alternative evaluative process is found, the replacement will likely be of even greater import, demanding even greater accountability.

Whether preparing for the visit of an accrediting agency or some successor assessment process, the academic library is best served if it concentrates on serving well the information needs of its community. In order to deliver effective information service, the library needs to put in place the following essential elements:

PLANNING that begins with ongoing analysis of user needs, that translates those needs into a responsive mission statement with defined goals and specific maintenance and project objectives to meet user needs.

ORGANIZATION that enables the users to identify, obtain, and utilize the information necessary to support their needs at optimum cost to the community.

STAFFING that is interactive with the user community, committed to the purposes and philosophy of its academic community, and reflective of the best in information theory and practice, supportive of change.

EVALUATION that employs routine and special studies to measure effective utilization of resources and the impact of services on users.

COMMUNICATION that encompasses routine and special reports to the user community and external agencies, and effective "intelligence" mechanisms to monitor changes in the user community.

FUNDING to plan for and procure sufficient resources to maintain ongoing services and to research, develop, and implement new information technologies and services.

A library that puts these elements in place will be prepared for an accreditation agency visit or any other assessment process, because it will be delivering effective information service and its user community will know it.

Reader Evaluation Form

To enable us to identify your needs and improve our counsel, the authors would like to hear about your ideas and experiences. You may choose to respond to one, some, or all of the checklist items or tell us in your own words about your needs.

I used the handbook to help my library prepare for an accreditation review.   YES   NO

The handbook was related to key accrediting issues in my library.   YES   NO

The handbook contents are easily understood.   YES   NO

The handbook was used for purposes other than an accrediting review, e.g., reviewing performance measures, developing a mission statement. If YES, please describe.   YES   NO

_____

_____

What else should be in the handbook? What topics, experiences, worksheets, or reference materials should be included?

_____

_____

What accrediting review experience would you like to share with us that will enable us to improve the handbook?

_____

_____

_____

Your name/institution/address

_____

_____

_____

Send to: Patricia Ann Sacks
          Cedar Crest and Muhlenberg College Libraries
          (FAX) (215) 821-3511 Internet pasacks@max.muhlberg.edu

          Sara Lou Whildin
          Delaware County Campus, Pennsylvania State University
          (FAX) (215) 892-1359 Internet slw@psulias.psu.edu

Patricia Ann Sacks, director of libraries at Muhlenberg and Cedar Crest colleges, has extensive experience with accreditation in libraries. She chaired the ACRL Standards and Accreditation Committee from 1976 to 1978 and 1981 to 1985. She has been a member of over 20 visiting teams for the Middle States Association, and has chaired Cedar Crest College's campus-wide self-study process for its 1983 and 1993 reaccreditation reviews.

Sara Lou Whildin, head librarian at Penn State University's Delaware County campus, has been involved in a number of planning and assessment activities, including chairing the Campus Strategic Planning Committee. She holds an MLS from the University of Pittsburgh and is a member of Beta Phi Mu.